Praying
God's
Heart

Prayers That Make a Difference

Alvin VanderGriend

Foreword by Dave Butts

PRAYERSHOP
PUBLISHING

Terre Haute, Indiana

PrayerShop Publishing is the publishing arm of Harvest Prayer Ministries and the Church Prayer Leaders Network. Harvest Prayer Ministries exists to transform lives through teaching prayer.

Its online prayer store, www.prayershop.org, has more than 600 prayer resources available for purchase.

ISBN: 9781935012153

1 2 3 4 5 6 | 2015 2014 2013 2012 2011 2010

Acknowledgments

Thanks . . .

To my wife and loving life-partner, Carolyn, for her support and patience during the long hours of my writing and for the momentous investment she has made in my life.

To the members of my support group: Greg Bode, Ron Hendricks, Dave Meyers, and Duane VanderGriend, who prayed for me and held up my sagging arms through months of writing.

To Doug Kamstra, Scott Roberts, and Gert Els, who read the manuscript and who made many valuable suggestions.

To prayer groups led by Phama Woodyard and Eldean Kamps, who read several of these devotional chapters and gave me valuable feedback.

To David Butts and the staff of Harvest Prayer Ministries, who believed I could write another book on prayer and who prayed faithfully for me as I prepared this manuscript.

To Jon Graf and PrayerShop Publishing for helping to make this a better book, for their marketing savvy, and for their commitment to the prayer-publishing ministry.

To the hundreds of authors, pastors, and teachers from whom I have learned so much of what I know today about intercessory prayer.

Above all, to the Lord Jesus Christ and the Holy Spirit, who inspired me and who heard my pleas for help with the words, sentences, and ideas that have gone into this book.

Contents

Foreword

It may sound strange, but as I picked up the manuscript for *Praying God's Heart* and looked at the titles of the chapters I got really excited. *At last,* I thought, *a practical, devotional approach to intercession that will deal with the real issues that face people who want to grow in intercessory prayer.* The purpose of intercession, its part in the plan of God, mistakes made by intercessors, listening prayer, spiritual warfare, and so much more is covered in this powerful new book by my friend Alvin VanderGriend.

More than twenty years ago, God brought Alvin into my life as friend, co-laborer, and, in so many ways, a mentor in the area of prayer ministry. I'm not surprised that his prolific pen has turned to the issue of intercessory prayer. Many of our discussions over the years focused on questions related to praying for others. In this amazing devotional book, Alvin not only answers those questions, but gives us opportunity put into practice what we are learning.

Virtually every Christian I know would like to pray more effectively. Especially as they pray for God to move in families, churches, and even nations, they want to know that their prayers are being used to bring about the purposes of God. This book is an answer to those desires! Good theology on prayer is coupled with practical instruction that will result in more effective prayers.

I believe today that God is highlighting intercession in the life of the church. It isn't that other aspects of prayer are not important.

They certainly are vital for a balanced prayer life. But God is calling the church to intercession as a means of releasing His power today, particularly in reviving the Body of Christ and finishing the task of world evangelization. The book you hold in your hands will be used greatly by the Lord in raising up an army of intercessors to accomplish His purposes in our day!

Dave Butts
Chairman, America's National Prayer Committee

Preface

This is a book about *intercession*—a form of prayer in which we pray for other persons and for kingdom causes. I am fully aware that prayer is more than intercession. A robust prayer life will always include adoration, thanksgiving, confession, petition, and submission. I have expanded on these elements of prayer in my two other devotional books: *Love to Pray* and *The Joy of Prayer*. In this devotional I am focusing primarily on intercession.

The *purpose* of this book is to expose from the Bible what God meant intercession to be and to help you translate these biblical truths into fruitful prayer practices. It is my hope and prayer that *Praying God's Heart* will help you grow strong in prayer and realize your full God-ordained potential as an intercessor.

Intercession is *important* to God. It is one of the greatest things we can do for God, for our churches, and for those for whom we pray. Intercession is a way of co-laboring with God. He doesn't need our prayers but He counts on them in advancing His kingdom and shaping history. Watchman Nee said of prayer that it is "None other than an act of believers working together with God."[1]

Intercessory prayer is neither simple nor easy. Ole Hallesby contends that "the fine and difficult art of . . . intercession is undoubtedly the most difficult of accomplishments. . . . Intercessory prayer is the finest and most exacting kind of work that it is possible for me to perform."[2] This book will help you wrestle with and get a grip on this fine and "most exacting kind of work."

Praying God's Heart is not just a book to read. You can't learn to pray simply by reading a book. This book will challenge you to think about prayer, to practice prayer, and to make some new long-term prayer commitments. There is no other way to develop an effective intercessory prayer life.

Be patient with yourself as you read this book. Growth in prayer does not come quickly and easily. God doesn't expect you to become a giant intercessor overnight. He understands your limitations. And don't feel like you have to intercede like anyone else. Learn from others, but try to develop a prayer style that is your very own. God will be pleased with the progress you make. As you make gains in intercessory prayer, He will count on you more and more. You will be making a greater and greater difference in people's lives and in the kingdom of God.

Alvin J. VanderGriend

Three Ways to Use This Book

Using this book with a **prayer group**

My primary reason for writing *Praying God's Heart* is to help existing prayer groups pray more effectively. To make this happen I suggest the following:

Before each meeting, prayer group members should read one devotional chapter and react personally to the "Think About" questions. Write down your thoughts in answer to these questions.

At the prayer meeting, spend about ten minutes reviewing the devotional chapter and sharing your thoughts on the questions. Spend the rest of your time in prayer. Try to make use of the "Pray About" suggestions in your prayer time.

Between your meetings, try the "Act On" suggestions. Pray for each other and ask God to help you grow stronger in prayer.

At the next meeting, share what you have learned from the "Act On" prayer activity and any evidences of growth in prayer.

Using this book **by yourself**

Praying God's Heart will also help individual believers learn to intercede more effectively. Here are my suggestions if you are using this book on your own:

Go through the devotional at a comfortable pace, but don't rush it. Take time to think through what you are learning and to apply it in your personal prayer life.

Write out brief answers to the "Think About" questions.

Use the "Pray About" suggestions in your personal prayer times. Let the Spirit help you expand on them.

Try some or all of the "Act On" suggestions.

Share important things you are learning with a family member or friend. You may even want to ask that person to pray that you will grow stronger in prayer.

Using this book in a **study group**

There is a lot to be learned about intercession. It's worth studying. Here are my suggestions if you are using this book in a study group:

Determine your pace based on the size of the group and the time you have available for each study session. You should be able to deal with up to three devotional chapters in a one-hour session.

Before the class session, participants should read the devotional chapters to be studied and write down answers to the "Think About" questions.

In the class sessions, go through each chapter picking up on key ideas and getting responses to the questions. If the group is larger than ten, try dividing into smaller groups for part of the session. Give these small group members a chance to share feedback or pose questions to the whole group.

In the class sessions, plan for prayer times that will allow members to make use of the "Pray About" suggestions. You might want to do these prayer times in smaller groups too.

Encourage group members to try the "Act On" activities on their own *after* the class.

At the next meeting, invite participants to report on any prayer growth experiences during the last week.

CHAPTER 1

When We Pray, God Works

I tell you the truth, anyone who has faith in me will do what I have been doing. He will do even greater things than these, because I am going to the Father. And I will do whatever you ask in my name, so that the Son may bring glory to the Father. You may ask me for anything in my name, and I will do it. —John 14:12–14

I first heard the phrase "when we pray, God works" when I was visiting a "praying" church in Houston, Texas. I had spent the day learning everything I could about that church's effective prayer ministry. I ended the day by interviewing the pastor and asking him what they were learning about prayer. I will never forget his answer. He said, what we learned is that "when we work, *we* work; when we pray, *God* works!"

"When we pray, God works!" What a simple way to describe intercessory prayer and to explain its purpose. Augustine wrote, "Prayer is to intercede for the well-being of others before God." Prayer is God's plan. God initiated intercession so He could work on earth in the way He wanted to, in response to prayer. By means of intercessory prayer He invites us to labor with him for the well-being of others. Prayer did not happen because people wanted things from God and decided to plead with Him for them. Prayer is not a human strategy for acquiring things. Nobody thought it up. Intercessory prayer is God's way of giving us a stake in His kingdom building work. He takes the initiative but involves us through prayer and our ministry activities. As we do our part—asking in His name and stepping out in ministry—He does His part.

Jesus reinforced this co-laboring concept of prayer for His disciples in the last week of His life on earth. It happened shortly after He told His disciples that He was going to leave them. They, understandably, were disconcerted by the thought of His leaving and by having to carry on without Him. Jesus calmed their troubled hearts by telling them how they would be able to carry on. He said, "Anyone who has faith in me will do what I have been doing. He will do even greater things that these." In other words, Jesus was saying, "You will be able to minister effectively after I leave." And here's why! "I am going to the Father. And I will do whatever you ask in my name." In other words, they would ask, and He would act. That's co-laboring, co-laboring by prayer.

Co-laboring with God—we pray, He acts—is the only really effective way that we can do the works of God. It's an effective way to work because the enthroned Son of God is the major player in this partnership. He is at the right hand of the Father and is in charge of all earthly operations. He is almighty, all wise, and pure love. Because He is almighty there is nothing He cannot do in answer to prayer. Because He is all wise He never makes a mistake in answering our prayers. Because He is pure love His answers will always reflect that love. He wants us to ask so that He can act in His might, in accord with His wisdom, and out of love in response to our asking. Our intercessory prayers trigger His powerful, wise, and loving way of working to build His church.

In Jesus' words to His disciples we see how and why intercessory prayer is so critically important. To His disciples, feeling inadequate to carry on without him, Jesus did not say, "You can do it. I have trained you. Just hang in there and work hard." Hard work is not the key to effective ministry. Neither did Jesus say, "Don't worry. I will be on the throne of the universe. I know what needs to happen. I will see that what needs to get done will get done, because I am God." Jesus didn't promise that He would make things happen while they, prayerlessly, sat around and waited for Him to act. Instead Jesus committed Himself to action in response to their prayers so that they could minister effectively. He brought *their working* and *His working* together, and He connected them by prayer. He made prayer the key to effective ministry. Without prayer they would be helpless. With prayer they would be effective, because He would be working with them.

Jesus also made it clear that their prayers would be combined with ministry. He promised that they would be able to do what He had been doing and "even greater things" than He had done. Think of what that means! During His days on earth Jesus healed the sick, cast out demons, multiplied bread and fish to feed thousands, stilled storms, and raised the dead. He drew large crowds, spoke with unparalleled brilliance, boldly tackled corruption in the temple, and stood up against the most powerful leaders of the day. Would they be able to do all those kinds of things? The answer is yes, they could, and they did. Those first disciples took Jesus' words to heart. They really prayed! And they really worked! They did the "greater things" that Jesus talked about. They spoke to great crowds. They stood up to the leaders who challenged them. They planted a church that lived by prayer and ministered with power. They prayed for signs and wonders, and Christ responded in power. They saw thousands come to faith. In the years that followed they were accused of turning the world upside down. They really turned it right side up.

Praying disciples are working disciples. When they pray and work, Jesus works in and through them, and great things happen.

The disciples' prayers, to be effective, had to be prayers in Jesus' name. "In Jesus' name" is not a pass code to get us into heaven's throne room. A prayer in Jesus' name is a prayer that is in accord with His will. It's what Jesus would have prayed were He physically present. They were able to pray in His name because they had His mind and His heart. When we truly want what God wants and turn such desires into prayer, those prayers will be prayers in Jesus' name. When the Spirit of truth lives in us and makes God's will known to us, we will pray in Jesus' name. Praying in Jesus' name makes intercession work. Both our asking and the Father's giving depend on it. Such prayers will not be prayers for special favors related to worldly comforts or personal pleasures. They will be prayers by which God's grace is released in the lives of those we pray for.

Finally, it needs to be said that Jesus didn't make this promise just to His twelve disciples. When He said, "Anyone who has faith in me will do what I have been doing," He was including you, if you are a believer, and me and about two billion other believers in the world today. What a great and far-reaching plan. Imagine what would happen in the world today if all two billion of us stepped out into works of service and, at the same time, asked Him to work in and through us. Would that be world-changing or what? That is what Jesus had in mind when He spoke these words. That is how He intends to "bring glory to the Father." In Jesus' way of thinking we are not just believers; we are His praying servants doing great works as He works His works in us. We are intercessors accomplishing His will and releasing His power and love in the world.

If you are one of the anyone-who-has-faith-in-me persons of whom Jesus spoke, then you need to be on the lookout for places where Christ wants and needs to work. Is there a child who needs to be spiritually formed, a friend who needs encouragement, or a neighbor who needs Christ? If you pray, Christ will work! Are there spiritual leaders who need to be uplifted, fellow believers who need empowerment, or a church that needs to be revived? If you pray, Christ will work! Do you know of an anxious person who needs peace, a lonely person who needs befriending, a stranger who needs to be invited in, or a hungry person who needs to be fed? If you intercede, Christ will work; He will work in you and through you. You will be doing the kinds of things that Christ did. You will be doing them in His power. *You will be co-laboring with God.* With this promise Christ is placing the powers of heaven at your disposal. What a huge and important responsibility! What an awesome privilege!

Something to **Think** About

• How do you react to the idea that, if you are an intercessor, Christ places the powers of the heavenly world at your disposal?

• Why must disciples who pray work? Why must disciples who work pray?

• Why does Jesus not answer prayers that are not in His name?

Something to **Pray** About

• *Praise* God for the wisdom, power, and love with which He answers our prayers.

• *Thank* God for including you in His design for governing the world.

- *Ask* God to help you pray in His name.
- If prayer has been primarily a way for you to try to get special favors from God, *confess* that and seek God's forgiveness.
- *Commit* yourself to prayers that lead to work, and work that flows from prayer.

Something to **Act** On

Ask Jesus to reveal to you what He would pray were He in your place. Then turn what you know or think to be His will into a prayer in His name. Trust that Jesus has heard your prayer, and envision His mighty, wise, and loving response.

CHAPTER 2

Intercession, Prayer Born Out of Love

*"You have heard that it was said, 'Love your neighbor and hate your enemy.' But I tell you: Love your enemies and pray for those who persecute you, that you may be sons of your Father in heaven. He causes his sun to rise on the evil and the good, and sends rain on the righteous and the unrighteous. —*Matthew 5:43–45

*I speak the truth in Christ—I am not lying, my conscience confirms it in the Holy Spirit—I have great sorrow and unceasing anguish in my heart. For I could wish that I myself were cursed and cut off from Christ for the sake of my brothers, those of my own race, the people of Israel. . . . my heart's desire and prayer to God for the Israelites is that they may be saved. —*Romans 9:1–3, 10:1

Intercessors may love to pray but they also pray because they love. They lovingly invest time and energy interceding in behalf of others. If we define intercession with a love spin we might say it is a love-motivated plea, to a love-giving God, in behalf of love-needy persons, who live in a love-starved world. Love is the motivating force in all true intercession. Intercession is not simply a dispassionate communiqué in order to ask God to do something for others. It is a self-giving ministry of love and care for the benefit of others that releases God's grace into their lives.

Intercession is prayer born of love. It is the very nature of love to give. If we truly love people we will want for them more than we are capable of giving them. For the intercessor this loving desire leads to prayer in their behalf. Prayer is a way to bring God into the lives of others so that He will do for them what they cannot do for themselves.

Jesus brought intercessory prayer and love together in the Sermon on the Mount when He charged His hearers: "Love your enemies and pray for those persecute you" (Matthew 5:44). The two phrases in that sentence do not describe two different activities but rather one activity in two different ways. In other words, one way to love another person, even an enemy, is to pray for them. Or to reverse that idea, prayer for another person is a gift of love. Intercession is love on its knees.

The apostle Paul was a love-motivated intercessor. Burdened for the people of Israel he experienced "great sorrow and unceasing anguish in [his] heart," to the point of being willing to be "cursed and cut off from Christ for the sake of [his] brothers, those of [his] own race" (Romans 9:2–3). Motivated by that "great sorrow and unceasing anguish" he prayed, "My heart's desire and prayer to God for the Israelites is that they may be saved" (Romans 10:1). That's intercession birthed in a heart of love.

A Canaanite woman prayed a prayer one day that was born out of love. She came to Jesus crying out, "Lord, Son of David, have mercy on me! My daughter is suffering terribly from demon possession" (Matthew 15:22). Her pleas, which Jesus eventually granted, were motivated by a deep, loving concern for her suffering child. Her pleas represented the truest kind of intercession—a passionate request born of love.

Moses' pleas for the people of God in their wilderness journeys were also born of compassion. After Israel had sinned against the Lord by worshiping a golden calf, Moses pleaded in their behalf: "'O Lord,' he said, 'why should your anger burn against your people. . . . Turn from your fierce anger; relent and do not bring disaster on your people'" (Exodus 32:11–12). The next day, in a desire to make atonement for their sin, Moses went back to the Lord and said, "Oh, what a great sin these people have committed! They have made themselves gods of gold. But now, please forgive their sin—but if not, then blot me out of the book you have written" (Exodus 32:31–32). I can't imagine a greater human love than that. Can you? A willingness to be blotted out of God's book of life—for the sake of people who deserved to be punished? It was intercession born out of love.

Jesus' prayers are no doubt the high point of love-motivated intercession. Just before His arrest Jesus prayed for His disciple's protection, for their sanctification, and for their complete unity (John 17)—all prayers that reflect His loving concern for them; all kingdom prayers. The next day, nailed to the cross, Jesus prayed for those who crucified Him, "Father, forgive them, for they do not know what they are doing" (Luke 23:34). Today Jesus, at the Father's right hand, continues to intercede for us and all His people out of a heart filled with love. Because of His love-filled prayers we live in the confidence that nothing "will be able to separate us from the love of Christ" (Romans 8:39).

Love-motivated prayers for others are birthed from God's love for us and our love for God. They are prayers for what is on God's heart. With such prayers we step into God's loving concern for His children and His world. We join Him in His love ventures in the world. We become instruments of His love for people. Our loving prayers are like small streams of love that flow into His large river of love. When we pray in this way we not only participate in His love but we become like Him. Jesus reminded us that when we love our enemies and pray for those who persecute us, we are "sons of [our] Father in heaven" (Matthew 5:43–45).

God is willing and able to use us to touch the lives of others in gracious and loving ways. Intercessory prayer will "put us in their shoes." We will be drawn into their sorrows, and needs. We may not have the resources to bring healing, blessing, joy, and peace to them, but we know the One who does. He "is able to do immeasurably more than all we ask or imagine" (Ephesians 3:20). Through intercession we will release God's power and grace into other's lives. We will touch their lives in a way that non-intercessors cannot.

As we pray prayers propelled by love, we are one with Christ in His ongoing ministry of intercession. As members of His body, we share with Him in this ongoing work. Our prayers of intercession are an extension of His ongoing love-driven ministry of intercession.

When we truly love others we are committed to their ultimate good. Love means that we want them to be blessed "with every spiritual blessing in Christ" (Ephesians 1:3). We want them to have "everything [they] need for life and godliness" (2 Peter 1:3). We want them to enjoy the fruit of the Spirit and to be effective and fruitful. And knowing that God in His goodness is willing and able to grant such blessings, we willingly extend ourselves in prayer for those we love. That is intercession at its best. That is prayer born of love.

Something to **Think** About

• How will "love-motivation" affect *what* you pray for others? How will it affect the *depth of feeling* in your prayers for others? How will it affect your *relationships* with those for whom we pray?

• Love always desires the Father's best for those who are loved. What "best" things are you praying for others? Are these things the very best things?

• Try to think of a person who has hurt you or is hostile to you? Remembering that Jesus said, "Love your enemies and pray for those who persecute you," pray a love-motivated prayer for that person.

Something to **Pray** About

• All of Jesus' ongoing intercessory prayers for His people are motivated by His love. *Praise* Him for such a love.
• *Thank* God for love—His love for you, your love for Him, and the love that moves you to plead His grace for others.
• If some of your intercessory prayers have lacked heartfelt love, *confess* that to the Lord and ask His forgiveness.
• *Ask* God to help you pray for others out of a genuine, deep-seated love for them.
• *Commit* yourself to love-motivated intercessory prayer.

Something to **Act** On

Make a brief list of intercessory prayer concerns about which you feel very deeply. Reread Romans 9:1–3 and 10:1 above and think about Paul's deep concern for those he prayed for. Compare your desires to Paul's. Prepare to pray for your deep concerns by asking the Father to place *His* desires for these persons on *your* heart.

CHAPTER 3

Christ, the Ultimate Intercessor

During the days of Jesus' life on earth, he offered up prayers and peti-
tions with loud cries and tears to the one who could save him from death,
and he was heard because of his reverent submission. —Hebrews 5:7

Because Jesus lives forever, he has a permanent priesthood. Therefore he
is able to save completely those who come to God through him, because
he always lives to intercede for them. —Hebrews 7:24–25

Who is he that condemns? Christ Jesus who died—more than that, who
was raised to life—is at the right hand of God and is also interceding
for us. —Romans 8:34

No man ever prayed as Jesus prayed. E. M. Bounds wrote of Jesus' prayer life: "Prayer was the secret of his power, the law of
his life, the inspiration of his toil, and the source of his wealth, his
joy, his communion, and his strength."[1] Jesus was the only person
on earth whose prayer life never waned, even for a moment. No one
of us can ever make such a claim. I am sure that Jesus even lived up
to the high prayer standards that Paul set when he said, "Pray in the
Spirit on all occasions with all kinds of prayers and requests" (Ephesians 6:18) and "Pray continually; give thanks in all circumstances"
(1 Thessalonians 5:17–18).

For Jesus prayer was a *lifestyle*. It seems that He prayed at every major juncture and before every key decision in His life. He prayed in the morning (Mark 1:35). He prayed at night (Matthew 14:27), and sometimes all night (Luke 6:12). He prayed when He was alone (John 6:15), when He was with others (Matthew 11:15–26), and at public gatherings (Matthew 14:19). Scripture records eight actual prayers of Jesus, fourteen teachings of Jesus on prayer, eighteen references to Him praying, as well as three references to His intercessory prayer ministry after He ascended.* Every one of His prayers was faith-filled, heartfelt, and fervent. The writer of Hebrews compacts the essence of Jesus' prayer life into one sentence: "During the days of Jesus' life on earth, he offered up prayers and petitions with loud cries and tears to the one who could save him from death, and he was heard because of his reverent submission" (5:7). Jesus was *the* paramount pray-er.

Jesus Christ was also the *ultimate intercessor*. Intercession was a major part of His prayer life. It's from His intercessory prayer life and teaching that we especially want to learn in this devotional chapter. Many passages of scripture record Jesus' prayers for others. Matthew informs us that Jesus placed his hands on the little children that were brought to him and prayed for them (Matthew 19:13). Before raising Lazarus from the grave Jesus lets us in on the fact that He has been praying on the way there: "Father, I thank you that you have heard me. I knew that you always hear me" (John 11:41–42). After

---

*Jesus' prayers:** Lk. 10:21; Jn.10:41–42, 12:27–28, 17:1–26; Matt. 26:39, 27:46; Lk. 23:34, 46. **Jesus' teachings on prayer:** Mk. 11:25; Matt. 6:5–7, 6:8–13, 7:7–11, 9:37–38; Lk. 6:28; Mk. 9:29; Lk. 11:5–12; Matt. 18:19–20; Lk. 18:9–14; Matt. 21:21–22; Mk. 11:17; Jn. 16:23–24, 15:7. **Jesus praying:** Lk. 3:21; Mk. 1:35; Lk. 5:16, 6:12; Mk. 6:41, 46, 7:34, 8:6; Lk. 9:18, 29, 11:1; Matt. 19:13; Lk. 22:17–19, 22:32; Matt. 27:50; Lk. 24:30, 24:50; Heb. 5:7. **Christ's heavenly prayer ministry:** Jn. 14:16; Rom. 8:34; Heb. 7:25.

the Lord's Supper Jesus reinstates Peter with the reminder, "I have prayed for you, Simon, that your faith may not fail" (Luke 22:32). In His final prayer with His disciples Jesus intercedes for their protection, their joy, their sanctification, and their future place with Him in glory (John 17:9–17, 24). In the same prayer He intercedes that future believers will be one and that they may "also be in us [that is, in the Father and the Son]" (John 17:20–23). On the cross Jesus asks the Father to forgive those who crucified Him (Luke 23:34). Finally, forty days later, as He prepares to ascend to heaven, Jesus lifts up His hands and blesses those gathered (Luke 24:50). Intercession ran like a thread, maybe more like a rope, through the fabric of Jesus' life.

Many of Jesus' *teachings* were also on intercession. When the disciples asked Him to teach them to pray, He gave them what we now call the Lord's Prayer. What's important for us to understand here is that all the petitions of the Lord's Prayer are intercessory. The first three concern the great issues on God's heart: His glory, His kingdom, and His will. The next three are of paramount importance to our lives: His provision, His pardon, and His protection from the evil one. The "our" and "us" that run through the prayer are a constant reminder that when we pray these we are praying for ourselves *and* for others.

Jesus also knew that intercession would be a key factor in fulfilling God's kingdom plan. For starters, He had to claim the promise made to Him in Psalm 2:8: "Ask of me, and I will make the nations your inheritance, the ends of the earth your possession." His disciples would also have to become intercessors. In the middle of a teaching tour Jesus, concerned for spiritual harvests, challenged His disciples to "ask the Lord of harvest . . . to send out workers into his harvest field" (Matthew 9:37–38). When the disciples were afraid they couldn't do the work of ministry without Him, Jesus convinced them that they could do great things because they had prayer. He said, "I am going to the Father. And I will do whatever you ask in my name. . . ." (John 14:12–14). And, in the last evening before His arrest, Jesus urged them no less than six times to ask and receive. There is no doubt that Jesus intended intercession to be a major factor in the lives and ministries of Hhis disciples.

But Christ is the ultimate intercessor not only because He prayed on earth but even more because He continues His intercessory ministry in heaven today. Though Jesus' "cross work" is complete, his "throne work" goes on. The author of Hebrews reminds us that, "because Jesus lives forever, he has a permanent priesthood. . . . He always lives to intercede" (Hebrews 7:24–25). Similarly the apostle Paul notes, "Christ Jesus who died—more than that, who was raised to life—is at the right hand of God and is also interceding for us" (Romans 8:34).

Jesus' primary task as our enthroned intercessor is not simply to forward our prayer lists on to the Father. It is rather to intercede for the issues on the Father's heart: His glory, His kingdom, and His will, as well as for our provision, our pardon, and our protection. Christ's intercession guarantees all the plans and promises of God. That includes both our freedom from condemnation (Romans 8:34) and our complete salvation (Hebrews 7:25). Without Jesus' intercession the kingdom would never be established and we would be lost. It is a work that is absolutely crucial.

Our prayers of intercession are integrally related to Jesus' intercession. When we pray in His name we join Christ in His high priestly ministry, because to pray in His name is to pray as though Christ himself prayed. We are so united with Him in prayer that He prays in and through us, and we pray in and through Him. Christ authorizes His disciples on earth to represent Him, to be in a place for Him. He wants us to see things the way He sees them, to want what He wants, to love what He loves, and to do what He does—and out of that frame of reference to ask what He would ask. Such prayers will always relate in some way to the King's interests and desires. If our prayers miss the target, Christ will revise them and make them acceptable to the Father.

When we partner with the interceding Christ who is "seated at his [the Father's] right hand . . . far above all rule and authority, power and dominion" (Ephesians 1:20–21) we are also sharing in His authority. Our prayers get tied to His authority. This means that God having "raised us up with Christ and seated us with him in the heavenly realms" (Ephesians 2:6) allows us to pray with power, and promises to crush Satan under our feet, as we share in the authority of His throne. What a place! What a power! And all because our lives and our prayers are linked with the one who is the *ultimate intercessor.*

Something to **Think** About

• What would an intercessory *lifestyle* like that of Jesus look like today?

• What do you think has happened in your life because Jesus, together with other believers, has interceded for you along the lines of the six petitions of the Lord's Prayer? Be as specific as possible.

• Mother Teresa, reflecting on Christ's life in us, said, "Christ prays in me, Christ works in me, Christ thinks in me, Christ looks through my eyes, Christ speaks through my words, Christ works with my hands, Christ walks with my feet, Christ loves with my heart."[2] If that is true of you, how will it affect your prayers for others?

• To what extent does Jesus need to revise your prayers of intercession? Are you okay with that? What might be lost or gained as He does so?

Something to **Pray** About

• *Praise* Jesus Christ as the ultimate intercessor who has been interceding for you all your life.
• Give *thanks* that the Father always grants Jesus what He asks, which includes what you ask in His name, and sends the Holy Spirit to work out the answer.
• Identify your failures as an intercessor and *confess* them to the Lord. Go on to claim His complete forgiveness.
• *Ask* Jesus to make you more and more the intercessor He wants you to be.
• *Commit* yourself to an intercessory lifestyle.

Something to **Act** On

Read John 17:9–24 thoughtfully, noting the six things that Jesus prays for His disciples and for future believers. Pray those six things for persons you care about.

CHAPTER 4

The Spirit, Our Indwelling Intercessor

In the same way, the Spirit helps us in our weakness. We do not know
what we ought to pray for, but the Spirit himself intercedes for us with
groans that words cannot express. —Romans 8:26

And pray in the Spirit on all occasions with all kinds of prayer and
requests. With this in mind, be alert and always keep on praying for all
the saints. —Ephesians 6:18

One of the keys to a powerful intercessory prayer life is praying "in the Spirit." Dutch Sheets states boldly, "Without any
doubt the greatest single key to successful intercession is learning
to cooperate with the Holy Spirit, allowing him to be all he was
sent to be in us."[1] Happily, the Holy Spirit is both willing and able
to give us the prayer help that we need. But we do have to learn to
cooperate with Him.

Having acknowledged that "we do not know what we are to
pray," Paul asserts that "the Spirit helps us in our weakness." The
weakness of which he speaks is a weakness in prayer. The Greek
word for weakness (*asthenes*) is literally "strength-less." In calling
our prayer lives strength-less, Paul is not referring to an occasional
glitch in our praying but an underlying disability. When it comes to
prayer we are all disabled.

We know intuitively that Paul's assertion about our weak prayer lives is true. I don't think that I have ever met another Christian who didn't think his or her prayer life needed to be improved. But the question remains, how? There are so many distractions, and there is so little time in our busy schedules. Nothing is easier to neglect. The truth is we cannot develop a meaningful prayer life in our own strength. God must be in it, and He is ready and willing to help.

The Father is in the prayer-assistance business. He has appointed His Son, Jesus, to be our *enthroned* prayer assistant, and His Holy Spirit to be our *indwelling* prayer assistant. The Son does His assisting at the Father's right hand. The Spirit does His assisting from His place within our hearts. The Spirit is able to more than make up for what is lacking in our prayer lives. He is the all-sufficient helper. He knows all about us and all about prayer. He has the power to compensate for our weaknesses and the wisdom to enhance our prayer lives. And He wants to help us be strong in prayer. It's to God's advantage as well as our own.

There are several specific ways that the Holy Spirit helps us in intercession. One of the first things He does is to *sanctify* us. Since sin hinders prayer, sin has to be dealt with before we can pray. David acknowledged, "If I had cherished sin in my heart, the Lord would not have listened" (Psalm 66:18). The Holy Spirit cleanses our hearts and helps us gain victory over sin. Believers "do not live according to the sinful nature" says Paul, "but according to the Spirit," and he adds a few verses later, "by the Spirit you put to death the misdeeds of the body" (Romans 8:4, 13). The Spirit's sanctifying work is an important first step in helping us pray as we ought.

Second, the Spirit helps by *installing Christ* in our hearts. When Paul reports his prayers for the Ephesian believers he says: "I pray that out of his glorious riches he [the Father] may strengthen you with power through his Spirit in your inner being, so that Christ may dwell in your hearts through faith" (Ephesians 3:16–17). It is by means of the Spirit that Christ dwells in us. With Christ in our hearts we are able to think like Christ, love like Christ, and pray like Christ. We can intercede with His heart, His love, and His vision for the kingdom. As new creations in Christ (2 Corinthians 5:17) we have new-creature capabilities in prayer.

Third, the Spirit *motivates* us to pray what God wants prayed. Paul asserts that "the Spirit himself intercedes for us with groans that words cannot express." While it is not entirely clear whether it is the Spirit or the pray-er who groans, the fact that we have a personal interactive relationship with the Spirit means that both the Spirit and the person praying experience strong deep feelings. The "groans" of which Paul speaks may be understood as intense yearnings of the Father for the accomplishment of His purposes, yearnings that get birthed in our hearts by the Spirit. These yearnings become the grist of our intercessory prayers. For example, when believing parents pray that prodigal sons or daughters will return to the faith, they do so with the yearnings of the Father. When we pray for persecuted Christians or the surviving family members of martyred believers, we do so with deep groans of God. The Holy Spirit is the Father's agent in getting us to pray what is on His heart.

Fourth, the Spirit *enables us* to pray. When it comes to prayer we may be "strength-less" but we are not helpless. Paul reminds us that "the Spirit helps us in our weakness." The word "helps" is a Greek word that literally means "take hold of together with against." The Spirit is not so much praying *for* us as He is praying *with* us. He is "taking hold of prayer together" over "against" our weakness so that with His help we can pray as we should. We still do the praying, but we are not alone in doing it. Imagine a person trying to move a heavy log alone. The log is very heavy and he is too weak to lift it. But someone steps up to "take hold of it together" with him. Together they are able to move the log. It's like that with us and the Holy Spirit. What we are unable to do in our own strength, we can do with the help of the Holy Spirit.

When Paul tells us in Ephesians 6:18 to "pray in the Spirit," he is urging us to pray as the Spirit enables us to pray or to pray by the power and direction of the Spirit. In other words "pray in the Spirit" is not a command; it's an offer of help—help that is available for any praying believer, anytime, anywhere. The Holy Spirit is the great prayer helper.

Finally, the Spirit is eager to *guide us* in who and what to pray for. He is on the lookout for believers who will pray for what God wants to do. How practically does the Spirit do this? He may do it by giving you a *burden*—such a deep love and concern for a person or a cause that it weighs on you. He may do it by giving you an *unexpected thought*—a thought that breaks in so abruptly that you ask, "Where did that come from?" He may do it by giving you a *strong impression*—a sense that He wants you to pray about something so that He can act in response to your prayer. He may do it by making a *scripture verse come alive* in your heart so that you are reminded of a person or situation that needs prayer. The Spirit has control of our hearts and minds and emotions. He can cause a burden, thought, impression, or insight at anytime to guide us in prayer. If you are not certain that a prompting to pray is from the Spirit, then ask God for the wisdom that He promises to give "generously to all" who ask in faith (James 1:5). He *will* give the wisdom that He promised so you can be certain.

It is no wonder that Jesus strongly urged believers to pray for the Holy Spirit and promised that the Father in heaven would most certainly "give the Holy Spirit to those who ask" (Luke 11:13). If you have ever asked yourself, "What is the first step I should take in order to improve my prayer life," then here is the answer. Ask the Father for the Holy Spirit, trust that He gives you the Spirit, and then lean on the Spirit for the help He gives in every aspect of your prayer life. He is willing; He is able; and He will do it.

Something to **Think** About

- Compare the experience of being helped by a counselor, lawyer, doctor, or tax accountant to being helped by the Holy Spirit? What's similar? What's different?

- Review the five ways (above) that the Spirit helps us in our intercessory prayer lives. Which of the five "helps" have you already experienced? Which help do you most need to grow your prayer life?

- Jesus Christ is your *enthroned* prayer assistant; the Holy Spirit is your *indwelling* prayer assistant. What is different about the help that each gives? What is similar?

Something to **Pray** About

- *Praise* the Holy Spirit as the supreme "prayer helper."
- *Thank* God that the Spirit is always with you and in you (John 14:17) to help you intercede.
- If you have quenched the Spirit and failed to receive His help in prayer, *confess* that to the Father and seek His forgiveness.

- *Ask* the Father to strengthen your prayer life by filling you with His Holy Spirit.
- *Yield* yourself fully to the Spirit as He exerts His influence in you.

Something to Act On

Each time that you pray in the coming weeks stop at the beginning of your prayer time to invite the Holy Spirit to cleanse you, motivate you, strengthen you, guide you, and quicken the Christ-life within you. Continue in prayer with a consciousness that He is doing what you have asked.

CHAPTER 5

Prayer Is More for God than for Us

Now my heart is troubled, and what shall I say? "Father, save me from this hour?" No, it was for this very reason I came to this hour. Father, glorify your name!" —John 12:27–28

I will do whatever you ask in my name, so that the Son may bring glory to the Father. You may ask me for anything in my name, and I will do it. —John 14:13–14

We constantly pray for you, that our God may count you worthy of his calling, and that by his power he may fulfill every good purpose of yours and every act prompted by your faith. We pray this so that the name of our Lord Jesus may be glorified in you, and you in him."
—2 Thessalonians 1:11–12

I received a letter the other day from a person asking me to pray about a family problem. Along with that request came additional pages with forty-four more prayer requests, all of them for various aspects of personal and family life. Most of the requests were for good and legitimate concerns. This person was clearly seeing God as the source of all blessings and was asking me to pray for them. That was good! What was not so good was that all of the requests were "for them" with little apparent thought as to their value "for God."

This approach to prayer is typical of what we find in many churches today. Our bulletins are full of prayer requests that mention the things that we want God to do for us. We want Him to heal our diseases, relieve our distresses, bail us out of our problems, and provide us with plenty. William Barclay, commenting on this view of prayer, said, "One of the strangest things about prayer is that it can be the most selfish activity in the world. Prayer can be merely seeking to use God for one's own purposes."[1] But, intercession is not first of all about us; it is about God and His kingdom.

The problem is not that it is wrong to pray for healing, help, and blessings. We should pray for these things. In the Lord's Prayer, Jesus teaches us to pray, "Give us our daily bread" (Matthew 6:11). That is a prayer for God to supply our physical, material, and bodily needs. But the problem comes when the focus in prayer is primarily on us and what we want. What we are really doing when we pray that way is trying to get God to be our servant. But He is not our servant. He is our Lord and Master and we are His servants. Of course, He does bless us, help us, and even serve us. But, in doing so He does not relinquish headship. He blesses us out of love so that *we* may serve *His* purposes.

Intercessory prayer is more for God than for us. It is more a way for God to accomplish His purposes on earth than for us to get God to give us, or those we pray for, something. Jesus clearly thought first of God and His glory when it came to prayer. In a troubling moment He didn't immediately think of how the Father could help Him. He even said that He wouldn't pray, "Father, save me from this hour?" Instead, recognizing that His suffering was part of God's plan, He simply prayed, "Father, glorify your name!" (John 12:27–28).

On another occasion Jesus promised His disciples that if they would ask in His name He would do what they asked. But He didn't stop there. He went on to say that He would act in response to their prayers "so that the Son may bring glory to the Father" (John 14:13). In other words, their asking was not just to get His help or to be empowered for ministry. The ultimate reason for their asking and His acting was to glorify the Father. Jesus clearly viewed prayer as *for God* and *for* His glory.

Ole Hallesby affirms that the one grand-scale purpose of prayer is to glorify God. He says, "The fundamental law in prayer is this: Prayer is given and ordained for the purpose of glorifying God. Prayer is the appointed way of giving Jesus an opportunity to exercise His supernatural power of salvation. And in so doing he desires to make use of us. . . . We should through prayer give Jesus the opportunity of gaining access to our souls, our bodies, our homes, our neighborhoods, our countries, to the whole world, to the fellowship of believers and to the unsaved."[2] Intercession that flows from this way of thinking will no doubt be glorifying to God.

When we think of intercession as more *for God* than for us, all kinds of things will change. We will ask different questions. Instead of asking, "Where is the problem?" we will ask, "Where does God want to work?" Instead of asking, "What do *we want* from God?" we will ask, "What does *God want* for us and for those we pray for?" Instead of asking, "What will we gain?" we will ask, "How will God be glorified if He grants what I ask; how will He gain?" We will pray different kinds of prayers. We will pray less for relief and more for sufficient grace. We will pray less for comfort and more for spiritual growth. We will be less concerned with what He can do for us and more concerned for what we can do for Him. Intercession will become a way in which we co-labor with God to accomplish His will and bring in His kingdom. Intercessors yearn for God's work to be done.

Of course, intercession is not only for God. God has so linked us with Himself that what is *for* Him is also *for* us. The apostle Paul links both God's glory and the believer's glory to prayer. After reporting to the Thessalonians how he prays for them he says, "We pray this so that the name of our Lord Jesus may be glorified in you and you in him" (2 Thessalonians 1:11–12). The last phrase, "and you in him," is the surprise. With that phrase Paul is saying, "My prayers will bring glory not only to Christ, but also to you who belong to Christ." God's glory and the believer's highest good are secured by intercessory prayer at one and the same time.

Our intercessory prayers release God's rich blessings in the world—blessings that ripple on for many years, through many lives, and in many different forms. God is the first one to be blessed when we intercede, but not the last. When the lives of parents are touched through prayer, the blessing accrues to their children and grandchildren. When a pastor is blessed through intercessory prayer, his congregation is also enriched spiritually. When intercessors pray a friend to Christ, all that person's relationships are affected for the rest of his or her life. The hand that is moved when we pray is the hand of our loving, almighty, all-wise, everlasting Father. No wonder, then, that our intercessory prayers to the Father have such a huge ripple effect.

When we seek to orient all our prayers to what God is doing and plans to do, the Holy Spirit will always be there to help us. He will guide us to pray in line with the purposes of God. He knows what will bring glory to the Father and blessing to humankind, and He will guide us to pray along those lines. Satan will, of course, be there tempting us to make intercession a tool for special favors and personal advantage. If, however, we pray "in the Spirit" and "in Jesus' name," our prayers will always be, first of all, *for* God. They will be used to achieve God's purposes and will inevitably frustrate the devil and his purposes. That's what you want to see happen, isn't it?

Something to **Think** About

- How will your prayer life be affected if you always intercede with the awareness that prayer is more for God than for us?

- What does God most want to do in your life in response to prayer? In the lives of family members? In your church? In the world? What can you do to make sure that this awareness dominates your prayer life?

- What are some things that God is doing in the world today because you are interceding?

Something to **Pray** About

- God's glory is the sum total of all His attributes. *Honor* Him for the great, glorious, and wonderful God He is.
- *Thank* God for inviting you, together with all His children, to be involved in His glorious work through your prayers.
- If, in your intercessory prayer, you seldom think of God's glory, *confess* that as a wrong way to pray and *commit* yourself to turning that around.
- *Ask* God to make His hearts desires so clear to you that, in your intercessory prayers, you will be more concerned for what He wants than for what you want.

Something to **Act** On

As you begin to intercede for others, stop and ask God, "What will bring You glory in my family? In my church? In this world? Give God time to reveal His will through His Word and Spirit. Once you have a sense for what will bring God glory, pray for that.

CHAPTER 6

The Listening Side of Intercession

*After a long time, in the third year, the word of the LORD came to Elijah: "Go and present yourself to Ahab, and I will send rain on the land." . . . Elijah climbed to the top of Carmel, bent down to the ground and put his face between his knees. "Go and look toward the sea," he told his servant. And he went up and looked. "There is nothing there," he said. Seven times Elijah said, "Go back." The seventh time the servant reported, "A cloud as small as a man's hand is rising from the sea.". . . The sky grew black with clouds, the wind rose, a heavy rain came on. —*1 Kings 18:1, 42–45

*In the first year of his [Darius] reign, I, Daniel, understood from the Scriptures, according to the word of the LORD given to Jeremiah the prophet, that the desolation of Jerusalem would last seventy years. So I turned to the Lord God and pleaded with him in prayer and petition, in fasting, and in sackcloth and ashes. —*Daniel 9:2–3

*Do not pray for this people nor offer any plea or petition for them; do not plead with me, for I will not listen to you. —*Jeremiah 7:16

Intercession, like all true prayer, starts with God. God tells us what He wants us to ask so that we can ask what He wants, and then He in turn answers our prayer and accomplishes what He wills.

His part in this scenario is to reveal to us what to pray about. Our part is to listen and to pray about those things that He reveals. When it comes to prayer God initiates, we collaborate.

When Israel repented, following the drought they had brought on themselves through their worship of Baal, God promised to send them rain. He said to Elijah, "Go and present yourself to Ahab, and I will send rain on the land." On hearing that, Elijah did not presume that the rain would come whether or not he prayed. He presumed the very opposite, that he needed to pray in order to bring to pass what God was committed to do. So "Elijah climbed to the top of Carmel, bent down to the ground and put his face between his knees." The face-between-his-knees position was a posture associated with intense prayer. Elijah prayed intensely, not just once but seven times, before God's answer came. Elijah listened and then prayed for the promised rain. God heard and sent the rain He had promised.

Daniel also listened and prayed. He listened to the scriptures: "I, Daniel, understood from the Scriptures . . . that the desolation of Jerusalem would last seventy years." When Daniel discovered that the seventy years were nearly up, he didn't just twiddle his thumbs and watch for the end of the captivity. Instead, we read that he "turned to the Lord God and pleaded with him in prayer and petition, in fasting, and in sackcloth and ashes." Daniel didn't doubt that God would keep His promise to restore Jerusalem. He also didn't doubt that prayer was a necessary part of bringing it to pass.

Elijah and Daniel both listened to God first and then prayed. They based their prayers on what they had "heard." Elijah heard God speak directly. Daniel heard God speak through the scripture. They took God's revelation seriously. They took their prayer responsibility seriously. They understood the listening side of prayer.

Listening prayer is simply this: First, we listen, and then we pray.

There are several different ways that we can listen.

First, we can "hear" *directly from God*. When God the Father speaks, it is always through His Son and His Spirit. Of believers Jesus said, "My sheep hear my voice . . ." (John 10:27, NASB). Hearing Jesus' voice is direct hearing. Paul calls the Holy Spirit the "Spirit of . . . revelation" (Ephesians 1:17). This Spirit of revelation dwells within us and is able to reveal what God wants to say directly to our hearts and minds. What we "hear" from God shapes our prayers, so that we know what to pray.

By listening we may even learn *when not to pray* for something. At a time when the spirit of unrighteousness reigned in Israel, God said to Jeremiah, "Do not pray for this people nor offer any plea or petition for them: do not plead with me, for I will not listen to you." The link between our prayers and God's actions is so tight that God doesn't want us praying for things that He definitely doesn't want to do. Though He probably won't speak to you as decisively as He did to Jeremiah, He may at times put a check in your spirit when you start praying for someone or something. When that happens, it may be time to change your prayers.

Second, we can "hear" as Daniel did *from the scriptures*. We may not know dates and times as he did, but we know from the scriptures that God wills to glorify His name in the earth, extend His kingdom, build His church, disperse the gospel, call workers into the harvest fields, defeat the powers of darkness, and reach out in love to a lost and hurting world. Knowing from the scriptures that God purposes to do these things should motivate us to pray passionately and persistently for their accomplishment. The better we know scripture, the better we will know God's purposes. The better we know God's purposes, the better we will pray.

Third, we also know how to pray in accord with God's will because we have *the mind of Christ*. As we mature in the faith, are filled with the knowledge of God's will (Colossians 1:9), and the eyes of our hearts are enlightened (Ephesians 1:16), we develop the ability to think like Christ. When Christ lives in us to the point where we think His thoughts, feel His emotions, will His will, and embrace His kingdom vision, then we will be able to pray with the mind of Christ. We will pray what Christ would pray were He in our place, and we will be praying in Jesus' name.

The trouble with so much of our intercession is that we don't take the time to think about what God's will might be before we ask. We don't listen very well. We just rush into His presence with wants and wishes and requests. We are so busy talking *to* God that we don't have time to hear *from* God. If we don't bother to hear God first, we shouldn't be surprised if our prayers misfire.

If you really want to make gains in listening prayer, here are a few practical suggestions that may help.

Stop and listen before you pray. Give the Holy Spirit the time and space to teach you how to pray in behalf of others. Put the burden of knowing how to intercede back on God. He can handle it.

Ask God to reveal His will to you before you intercede. *Invite* the Spirit to teach you what to pray for. He doesn't usually speak uninvited.

Pray the scriptures. Read the Bible with an ear tuned to the Holy Spirit. You will find Him teaching you when and where and how to apply the truths you are reading through your prayers.

Question the prayer requests you receive from others. You don't always have to pray what others ask you to pray. You always want to pray what God wants you to pray. There may be a difference.

Memorize and learn Bible passages that plainly reveal God's will and pray them regularly. Start with the Lord's Prayer and the prayers of Paul in Colossians 1:9–13, Philippians 1:9–11, and Ephesians 1:16–22 and 3:15–19. Then go on to other passages like the "add to" verses of 2 Peter 1:5–8, the "pursue" recommendations of Paul in 1 Timothy 6:11, and the "clothe yourselves" commands of Colossians 3:12. If we ask for these kinds of spiritual qualities and graces, our prayers for others will always be on target.

Something to **Think** About

• Elijah and Daniel both pleaded for sure things—sure because God had said they would happen. What "sure things" might God want you to pray for?

• How much of your prayer times are given to talking to God? Listening to God? Are you satisfied with the balance? What can you do if you are not?

• What concerns you more when you pray: getting what you ask for or seeing God's will done?

• Have you ever asked the Spirit to put a "check" in your spirit if what you were praying for was not His will? Is this something to consider in the future?

Something to **Pray** About

• *Praise* God that He is a "revealer." He brings us into His governance of the world by revealing His will and inviting us to pray about it.
• *Thank* God for the scriptures through which He clearly reveals His

love for you and His purposes in history.

• If you have talked too much and listened to little in your prayers, that may be something to clear up with God by means of *confession.*

• *Ask* the Spirit to help you develop the listening side of prayer.

• *Commit* yourself to any of the practical suggestions above that will help you be a better listener.

Something to **Act** On

Try out the five practical suggestions on pages 45-46. If you find one or more really helpful, then make a commitment to continue in that practice.

CHAPTER 7

God Seeks Intercessors

I have posted watchmen on your walls, O Jerusalem; they will never be silent day or night. You who call on the LORD, give yourselves no rest . . . till he establishes Jerusalem and makes her the praise of the earth.
—Isaiah 62:6–7

I looked for a man among them who would build up the wall and stand before me in the gap on behalf of the land so I would not have to destroy it, but I found none. So I will pour out my wrath on them and consume them with my fiery anger, bringing down on their own heads all they have done, declares the Sovereign LORD. —Ezekiel 22:30–31

So he said he would destroy them—had not Moses, his chosen one, stood in the breach before him to keep his wrath from destroying them.
—Psalm 106:23

Intercessors are important to God. He seeks intercessors. In fact, He counts on them. S. D. Gordon, in his classic *Quiet Talks on Prayer*, said: "The great people of the earth today are the people who pray. I do not mean those who talk about prayer; nor those who say they believe in prayer; nor yet those who can explain about prayer; but I mean those people who *take* time and *pray*. . . . They are the people that put prayer first, and group other items in life's schedule around and after prayer. . . . These are the people who are doing the most for God; in winning souls; in solving problems; in awakening churches; . . . in keeping the old earth sweet awhile longer."[1]

There is one intercessor who the Father counts on above all others. Jesus Christ, who "always lives to intercede" (Hebrews 7:25). His intercessory prayers undergird all the operations of the kingdom. They bring glory to the Father, bring salvation and security to the people of God, and build the church on earth. God's plan for history moves forward because Christ intercedes. He is the *ultimate intercessor.* However, He does not intercede alone. Our intercessory prayers in Jesus' name are drawn into His prayers and His prayers include ours. God counts on His Son to incorporate and reform our prayers.

A second intercessor that God counts on is the Holy Spirit. He is the *indwelling intercessor* whose primary intercessory activity is within us. Sent by the Father and the Son, the Spirit enables us to pray "on all occasions with all kinds of prayers and requests" (Ephesians 6:18). The Spirit puts God's burdens on our hearts and brings our prayers into line with God's will. God counts on the Holy Spirit to help us pray as we ought.

In Old Testament times God counted on a limited number of persons from the tribe of Levi to be priests to represent the people before Him. These priests were permitted to go where ordinary Hebrews were not permitted to go, into the very presence of God. Their role was essentially that of intercessors or "in-between-ers." Isaiah, however, predicted that a day would come when all of God's people would be called "priests of the LORD" (Isaiah 61:6). That day has arrived, says Peter. New Testament believers are "a royal priesthood" (1 Peter 2:9). That means we are all priests. We are all officially appointed as intercessors. The privilege of access to God, once very limited, has now been opened to all of us. We are given this access not only to pray for ourselves, but also to pray for others—to be intercessors. God counts on our prayers to mediate His blessings to others and carry forward His love-plan for the world.

God, it seems, has always been using intercessors and their prayers in shaping history. God used Moses' prayers to keep His wrath from destroying Israel. God used Daniel's prayers to return Israel to the Promised Land. God used Elijah's prayers to reprimand Israel by stopping and later restarting rainfall in the land of Canaan. To assure that there would always be intercessors to bring about His purposes, God even arranged to have watchmen posted on the walls of Jerusalem and mandated them to "call on the LORD," and "never be silent day or night." Today, through the work of His Son and His Spirit, God has arranged to have about two billion "watch persons" posted throughout the nations of the earth to "call on the Lord" and "never be silent day or night." That is the group that you and I are part of.

Lack of intercessory prayer can also lead to divine reversals. At a dire point in Israel's history, God looked for an intercessor among them who would "build up the wall and stand before me in the gap on behalf of the land so that [He] would not have to destroy it." But God found no one He could count on that day, so He said, "I will pour out my wrath on them and consume them with my fiery anger" (Ezekiel 22:30–31). If God had found an intercessor to stand in the gap that dark day, the future of Israel would have been different. Today, there is no such lack. There is an intercessor who stands in the gap pleading God's mercy for a sin-ravished world. That intercessor is Jesus Christ, and we stand with Him.

Intercessory prayer is cooperation with God. He chooses to have us cooperate with Him in order to bring His plans for the world to complete fruition. God could bypass us humans if He chose to do so. He is sovereign, almighty, and all-wise. He doesn't need our permission to act. But He has chosen to bring us in on the process and has prepared us to be intercessors through the work of His Son and His Holy Spirit.

Intercession is not optional. It is of extreme importance. Ole Hallesby is correct in calling prayer "a labor for which there is no substitute in the kingdom of God . . . the most important work we have to do." Later he underscores the effectiveness of prayer saying, "God takes immediate cognizance, therefore, of man's prayer in his government of the world. Something does take place as a result of man's prayer, which otherwise would not take place. In fact, as we have . . . seen, man's prayer is one of the most effective means by which God directs the world forward towards its goal, the kingdom of God."[2]

Even though intercessory prayer originates with God, God still counts on us and our prayers. We are part of the prayer cycle by which He accomplishes His work in the world.

Sometimes when I receive an e-mail asking for prayer, I hit "reply" and say, "Count on me!" When I say "count on me," I do not take that lightly. I always make a note of the prayer request and add it to my list of daily prayer prompts. It occurs to me now that I have never said "count on me" to the Father. But I think that I should. I realize that this is an awfully big promise to make. But I can do it, and you can do it too, because of the intercessory work of His enthroned Son and the work of His indwelling Spirit. God the Father is seeking intercessors He can count on. What do you think? Would you join me in saying to the Father, "Count on me"?

Something to **Think** About

- How do you react to extreme statements, such as "The great people of the earth today are the people who pray" and "Prayer is the most important work we have to do!"? Are these extreme, or are they right on?

• Can you think of a good reason why God has chosen to act in response to the prayers of intercessors and not to act, in ways He otherwise would have, if there was no intercessor?

• Do you think of intercessory prayer as a privilege or a responsibility? Explain.

Something to **Pray** About

• *Praise* Christ as the one and only *ultimate intercessor.*
• *Thank* the Holy Spirit for the help He gives you when you do not know how to pray as you ought.
• Identify and *confess* anything in your life that may be keeping you from being an intercessor who God can count on.
• *Ask* God to make you the intercessor that He wants you to be.
• *Ask* Him to help you know who to pray for, what to pray for, and why?

Something to **Act** On

Circle those areas on the following list that God can count on you to pray for. Add some of your own that are not on the list: family, friends, church, neighbors, a school, a social issue, government leaders, marketplace concerns, poor people, justice, missionaries, the media, a nation, ___*Luba*___ , ___*Nicy & Edward*___ ___*Denise J.* N K___

CHAPTER 8

Praying Kingdom Prayers

This, then, is how you should pray: "Our Father in heaven, hallowed be your name, your kingdom come, your will be done on earth as it is in heaven. . . . And lead us not into temptation, but deliver us from the evil one." —Matthew 6:9–10, 13

Another angel, who had a golden censer, came and stood at the altar. He was given much incense to offer, with the prayers of all the saints, on the golden altar before the throne. The smoke of the incense, together with the prayers of the saints, went up before God from the angel's hand. Then the angel took the censer, filled it with fire from the altar, and hurled it on the earth; and there came peals of thunder, rumblings, flashes of lightning and an earthquake. —Revelation 8:3–5

One of the most exciting discoveries that I ever made about prayer was that, when we are praying for ourselves [petition], if our hearts are right with God and we ask in accord with His will, God will give us what we ask (1 John 5:14–15). I wrote about this in my earlier devotional on prayer, *Love to Pray*. In an effort to personally claim that promise and receive God's riches, I made a list of seventy-five spiritual qualities and blessings mentioned in scripture—things I could be sure were "in accord with God's will." I understood these to be God's purposes in my life. I asked God for these things several times each week. What I found was that God, true to His word, heard and answered these prayers. Little by little these qualities and graces became more and more real in my life. God was answering because I was praying for what He wanted. I was praying kingdom prayers.

The same principle holds true when we pray God's purposes for other believers [intercession] if their hearts are right before Him. When we intercede in faith for *things that God purposes to do*, we can pray with absolute assurance that He hears and answers these prayers. They may not always be answered according to our expectations or on our timetables, but they will surely be answered. Our prayers contribute to what God is doing—building His kingdom.

The first three petitions of the Lord's Prayer speak more clearly to God's purposes in the world than any other passage of scripture. When Jesus taught His disciples to pray: "Our Father in heaven, hallowed be your name, your kingdom come, your will be done on earth as it is in heaven" (Matthew 6:9–10), He was teaching them to pray what was on the Father's heart. The three things that the Father most wants to see happen on earth are for His name to be glorified, for His kingly rule to be established, and for His will to be done fully and completely. These are the Father's grand-scale purposes. When we pray for them we are praying in accord with God's will. These are things that must happen and will happen. Jesus asked us to pray for them so the Father could make them happen in accord with our prayers.

When we pray the Lord's Prayer, we are not telling God what *we* are going to do. We are asking Him to do what only *He* can do. We are making bold prayers of intercession to an almighty God. Darrell W. Johnson, in *Fifty-Seven Words that Change the World*, notes: "The verbs of the Lord's Prayer, addressed to the Superior of superiors, *are in the imperative.* They are commands, not requests. Be hallowed! Be come! Be done! All in the command form. To pray the Lord's Prayer is to command—not to ask—but to command. . . . This may strike you as somewhat audacious. Who are we to speak to God in such a manner? What helps is to further know that the verbs in the first three petitions are in the *passive voice.* . . . The passive voice softens the tone. Instead of 'do it,' it is 'be done.' But the verbs are passive for a more fundamental reason. *Only God can do what we are asking to have done.*"[1]

Imagine for a moment that you are in the stands cheering on your favorite sports team. In the last minutes of the game your team has gained a slight advantage and it looks like they are going to win. You are on your feet, cheering and shouting for them to "go." We are challenging them to hold on, to be strong, and to do what they have to do to win. Your encouraging shouts are not pious wishes or hopeful pleas. They are urgent challenges to try and make it happen. They are, to put it grammatically, passive imperatives. When we pray the Lord's Prayer, our prayers are something like those urgent challenges. We are saying with a sense of great insistence, "Father, hallow Your name; advance Your kingdom; do Your will on earth. Make it happen, Lord!" And He will.

The Father loves to hear our prayers for His glory, His kingdom, and His will. He delights to answer such prayers. He has the ability to do what we ask. There is no way that the almighty sovereign God of the universe will ever let history come to an end without glorifying His name, establishing His glorious kingdom, and accomplishing His will fully and completely. In fact He is already doing these things, and the day will come when they will all be done on earth as perfectly as they are done in heaven. So pray them in faith; pray them with absolute confidence. You are contributing to the realization of His purposes! That's an exciting way to pray.

There are three other purposes we can pray for with equal certainty. We can pray for the *spread of the gospel*. Jesus declared, "This gospel of the kingdom will be preached in the whole world as a testimony to all nations" (Matthew 24:14). It's going to happen. When we intercede for the spread of the gospel, we confidently expect that our prayers are being answered. It cannot be otherwise. Often, when praying in this vein, the Spirit will lead us to pray for family members, friends, or neighbors who appear not to have a relationship with Christ.

Jesus also declared, "*I will build my church,* and the gates of Hades will not overcome it." (Matthew 16:18, emphasis added). The church is being built and some day it will be complete. When we pray, "Lord, build Your church as You said You would," we are praying in accord with God's will. God always hears such prayers. They will never be lost in a netherworld of divine forgetfulness. Among these will be prayers for our own local churches—prayers for growth in grace, for revival, and for effective outreach efforts.

In the book of Revelation, John tells us that the collective prayers of all the saints, gathered in the golden bowls before the altar, are mixed with the offering incense and go up before God. God's response to those prayers is to initiate the beginning of the end time with "peals of thunder, rumblings, flashes of lightning and an earthquake." In other words, our prayers usher in *the end of history* and the second coming of Christ. When we pray, "Come, Lord Jesus, come quickly," we are praying God's purposes. Our prayers are contributing to God's final solution to the problem of evil. We are co-laboring with God.

Many more prayers of this nature can be found in scripture, prayers that will allow us to touch the world for God. To pray this way is to pray in Jesus' name, for these are the very kinds of prayers that Christ presents to the Father every day. When we pray this way, we are united with God in His purposes. We are united with Christ in His ongoing intercessory ministry. What a great thing to be part of. This makes prayer really effective and really exciting, don't you think?

Something to **Think** About

- How important to God are intercessors who faithfully pray for the purposes of God?

- Do you hear many prayers of this nature? Why might these kinds of prayers be neglected today?

- What other things could you pray about with confidence that the outcome is certain? Think in terms of other grand-scale scriptural themes.

Something to **Pray** About

- *Praise* God for the wisdom and power with which He works out His plans.
- *Thank* God for His willingness to involve you, through your prayers, to fulfill His purposes on earth.
- If your prayers have been narrow and selfish, seldom touching on God's greater purposes, that may be something for which to seek God's *forgiveness.*
- *Ask* God to expand your prayer life to the point where you regularly pray for the things that are most important to Him.

Something to **Act** On

Try to pray for the six definite purposes of God mentioned in this chapter, plus others that you are aware of, each week. Pray them with the absolute conviction that God always hears and answers such prayers. Envision God acting in response to your prayers.

Be hallowed name
Be come   (Kingdom)
Be done   (will)

Spread of the gospel
Lord build your church
Come Lord Jesus, come quickly

CHAPTER 9

Leaving the Choice to God

Though he brings grief, he will show compassion, so great is his unfailing love. For he does not willingly bring affliction or grief to the children of men. —Lamentations 3:32–33

Three times I pleaded with the Lord to take it [a thorn in the flesh] away from me. But he said to me, "My grace is sufficient for you, for my power is made perfect in weakness." Therefore I will boast all the more gladly about my weaknesses, so that Christ's power may rest on me. —2 Corinthians 12:8–9

Is any one of you sick? He should call the elders of the church to pray over him and anoint him with oil in the name of the Lord. And the prayer offered in faith will make the sick person well; the Lord will raise him up. —James 5:14–15

Sometimes when we pray we don't know what God's will is for the specific situation we are praying about. We don't know if He will grant our request or not, so we pray and *leave the choice to God.* Even if we don't know His will, our prayers are still prayers of faith. By faith we are sure that God hears. By faith we are sure that He cares. By faith we are sure that God will do what is best. But we don't know what His best is. So we pray with hope. It may well be that most of our prayers are prayers of hopefulness.

It's okay to pray prayers of hopefulness. God is pleased with them. Prayers of hope are valid prayers, so long as we are not asking for things we know to be contrary to God's will. James reminds us, "Every good and perfect gift is from above, coming down from the Father of the heavenly lights" (James 1:17). Our hopeful prayers say to God that we look to Him as the great Provider. With such prayers we posture ourselves as His dependent children. God is honored in that!

God doesn't expect us to be perfect pray-ers. He does not expect us to know what is best in every situation and to always pray in that vein. He understands our limitations. He accepts our prayers, even if they are off target, because He accepts us as His dear children.

We can be sure that God, even if He doesn't give what we ask, will provide the grace to deal with what He allows in our lives and in the lives of those we pray for. Paul learned that when he prayed for the removal of a thorn in the flesh. God didn't remove the thorn as Paul asked, but God didn't say no either. He simply said, "My grace is sufficient for you, for my power is made perfect in weakness" (2 Corinthians 12:9). The same thing may be true when we pray for others. God may not actually say no. He just says, "My grace is sufficient. I will give them the strength to deal with that situation." And the truth is, God's all-sufficient grace is the best answer, even better than the relief that we may be asking for. If we keep that in mind, we will always be able to joyfully accept God's answer even if it isn't what we asked. We will see in His answers that "his power is made perfect in weakness."

There are many things we should ask for while we leave the choice to God. We should ask for *material blessings*. God is the source of all good gifts. He is pleased to have us ask Him for material blessings. Jesus taught us to pray, "Give us today our daily bread" (Matthew 6:11), and reminded us that the "Father in heaven gives good gifts to those who ask him" (Matthew 7:11)! Yet, when we ask for material blessings we are not always certain God will grant what we ask. Sometimes God chooses not to provide material or financial blessings. If He doesn't we know that He has His good reasons. His ways are higher than our ways. If He doesn't give the things we ask for, He always gives the grace to do without them.

God is pleased when we intercede for the *removal of trials and difficulties*. Jesus understood suffering. He knew what it was to flinch in the face of suffering, to be overwhelmed with sorrow, and to plead for relief (Matthew 26:38). He welcomes our prayers for delivery from trials and tribulations. But when we pray that God will remove difficulties, we cannot always be certain of the outcome. Trials are not always bad. Paul thought that sufferings were "not worth comparing with the glory that will be revealed in us" (Romans 8:18). Peter pressed home the reality that suffering and trials would prove the genuineness of faith and "result in praise, glory and honor when Jesus Christ is revealed" (1 Peter 1:7). So while God is pleased when we ask for the removal of trials and difficulties, He does not always do what we ask. Sometimes, in His infinite wisdom, He chooses to allow the suffering. If He does allow suffering, we can be sure that He has some higher goal in mind. When the Father allowed His Son to experience the agonies of Gethsemane, it was for a greater good—the good of the Son who through suffering accomplished our salvation and the good of all those for whom He died.

Scripture encourages us to pray for *physical and emotional healing*. David praises God as the Lord who "heals all your diseases" (Psalm 103:3). Jeremiah observes that God "does not willingly bring affliction or grief to the children of men" (Lamentations 3:33). James writes, "Is any one of you sick? He should call the elders of the church to pray over him and anoint him with oil in the name of the Lord" (James 5:14). Prayer for healing is prayer that takes God and His Word seriously. God surely wants us to pray for healing. Prayer promotes healing and healing stems from prayer. That doesn't mean, however, that God will heal every time we ask Him to. Sometime He allows sicknesses, disorders, and weaknesses for His purposes—purposes that we do not always understand. But with His purposes come His grace, grace that displays His power and His glory.

It is also right for us to pray that *life be prolonged*. Life is a precious gift of God. Paul thought so. He said, "For to me, to live is Christ" (Philippians 1:21). Physical life gives us opportunity to enjoy loving human relationships, to enjoy God's world, and to love and serve God. When death threatens, it's okay to pray for extended days on earth. Hezekiah pleaded with God for an extension of his life, and God gave him an extra fifteen years (Isaiah 38:1–5). God's main concern, however, is not to keep us alive, but rather to give us eternal life. So while it is surely good to pray for life to be prolonged when death threatens, we should always do so remembering that God's greatest gift is not physical life here on earth but eternal life in union with Christ.

Our intercessory prayers are important to God. Even when we don't know His will in a specific situation, and can't be sure of the outcome, He is pleased with our prayers. Our prayers demonstrate our dependence on Him. They confirm the trust and love relationship we have with Him. They give evidence of our love for the ones for whom we intercede. And they become the means by which God's all-sufficient grace is released in their lives. That's reason enough to pray fervently and persistently, even when we have to leave the choice to Him.

Something to **Think** About

- Do you sense that God is pleased when you pray for others? Why might God be pleased to have us ask even if He answers no?

- Have you ever been upset with God for not answering your prayers? What was the real problem?

- When you ask God to heal a loved one who is sick or has been injured, are you content to let God, in His wisdom, decide how to answer?

- What is better: getting what we ask for or getting the strength to deal with what we actually get? Why?

Something to **Pray** About

- *Praise* God as a prayer-hearing God who is always pleased when we come to Him with love-motivated prayers for others.
- *Thank* God for happily receiving and wisely revising your off-target prayers.
- If you have harbored any resentment toward God for not giving what you asked for, *confess* that to Him.
- *Ask* God to help you see and appreciate the wise way He responds to your intercessory prayers.
- *Commit* yourself to pray faithfully and fervently, even when you are not sure of God's will in a given situation.

Something to Act On

As you pray and leave the choice to God remember these things:

1. God is pleased to have you come.
2. God is pleased with your honest prayers even if they miss the mark.
3. God's answers will be laden with grace no matter what.

CHAPTER 10

The Conquering Power of Prayer

Joshua said to the LORD *in the presence of Israel: "O sun, stand still over Gibeon, O moon, over the Valley of Aijalon." So the sun stood still, and the moon stopped, till the nation avenged itself on its enemies.* —*Joshua 10:12–13*

"O our God, will you not judge them? For we have no power to face this vast army that is attacking us. We do not know what to do, but our eyes are upon you." As they began to sing and praise, the LORD *set ambushes against the men of Ammon and Moab and Mount Seir who were invading Judah, and they were defeated.* —*2 Chronicles 20:12, 22–23*

We know what power is. We use power tools and powered appliances, mow our lawns with power mowers, drive cars with horsepower-rated engines, and watch power point presentations. We know about nuclear power, wind power, solar power, political power, superpowers, and even willpower. But what really is power? Dictionaries describe it as a great force, ability, influence, or energy that is able to do, act, or produce.

So what do we mean by the conquering power of prayer? Let me start by explaining what we don't mean. The power of prayer is not a power inherent in prayer itself. There are no vibes or energies that flow to the person being prayed for when we utter words of prayer. All the power in prayer is God's power directed by the prayers of His people. Our prayers are powerful only when He hears and acts in response to them. When we pray, it is God who blesses; God who transforms; God who heals; and God who helps. Apart from God our prayers are nothing more than empty words.

It is God who acts and who acts in accord with His will and purposes. The power of prayer is not a power by which we coerce God to do what He doesn't want to do. It is not a way for us to overcome God's reluctance and to get Him to give us what we want. It is not a way to accomplish human plans or purposes that are not from God. Prayer brings to pass what God intends. The prayers that influence God are prayers in accord with His will, prayer that He has initiated in the first place. We do not by means of prayer use Him for our purposes. Instead He, by means of prayer, uses us for His purposes. We are His instruments.

The Bible is full of stories of powerful prayer. In response to Joshua's prayer, the sun stood still in the valley of Aijalon (Joshua 10:12–13). In response to Jehoshaphat's prayer, God delivered Israel from a powerful invading army (2 Chronicles 20). In answer to Hezekiah's prayer, God delivered His people from an Assyrian siege force (2 Kings 18–19). In answer to Daniel's prayer, Israel was restored to the Promised Land (Daniel 9). In response to the devoted prayers of the first New Testament followers, God poured out His Holy Spirit on the church (Acts 1:14, 2:1–11). Prayer is God's chosen way of working, in small ways or large.

The power of prayer is a power to accomplish God's will on earth. It is, first of all, *a power to bring blessing.* God wants to bless, but He wants to bless in response to our prayers. In order to accomplish this, He gives us the ability to intercede so that we can be involved in conferring His blessing on others. We become instruments by which His power and grace are bestowed on others or directed to their need. By means of prayer we co-labor with God as He imparts blessings on family members, friends, fellow believers, neighbors, and government leaders. We want what is best for them; that's why we pray. God also wants what is best for them. That's why He is pleased to hear and answer our prayers.

Intercessory prayer *is a power for social transformation*. We can have an impact far beyond our small personal worlds by means of intercession. We can influence cities and social environments. For example, God's people on their way to exile in Babylon were told to "seek the peace and prosperity of the city" to which they were being carried and to "pray to the LORD for it," with the understanding that "if it prospers, you too will prosper" (Jeremiah 29:7). The transformation that prayer can bring about in a city can also happen at a personal level, a family level, a church level, or in a small town. Nothing is too large or too small for God.

Intercessory prayer is a power given to believers *to stand against Satan*. As the apostle Paul describes our spiritual battle in Ephesians 6:10–17, he warns us of the devil's schemes, challenges us to stand firm and to be fully armored. And then urges us: "Pray in the Spirit on all occasions with all kinds of prayers and requests. With this in mind, be alert and always keep on praying for all the saints" (6:18). The call to "be alert" means, be aware that we are in a spiritual battle. "Always keep on praying for all the saints" in this context means to pray that all believers will be able to "stand against the devil's schemes." Without prayer believers can suffer harm. With prayer they will "be strong in the Lord and in his mighty power." Satan and every demon from hell know it well.

Intercessory prayer is *a power to change circumstances*. Prayer was a factor when God pushed back the waters of the Red Sea to make an escape route for His people. Prayer brought manna from heaven and water out of rocks. Prayer caused city walls to crumble and devil-inspired armies to flee. Prayer caused shackles to fall off, guards to sleep, and prison doors to open. When it comes to building His church and getting His will done on earth, God works in and through prayer. He stands ever ready to hear and answer prayer and change the circumstances that would hinder His purposes. If prayer was a factor in overcoming the herculean challenges recorded in scripture, then it can certainly change the small or great forces that come against us. I am sure you can think of some.

Intercessory prayer is a power that *can reach to every human need.* When it comes to meeting human need, we who pray are very limited. But through our prayers we can have an influence at many levels—physical, mental, social, spiritual, medical, and so on. We don't have to have the knowledge or expertise of specialists to affect these areas. God has that ability and His hand is moved through our prayers.

Prayer is powerful because *it can reach any place.* Prayer is not limited by space or time or distance. It gives us instant access into any home, any school classroom, any hospital, any government office, and any courtroom. Prayer cannot be kept out by *No Entry* signs. Prayer enters through walls, gets beyond locked doors, breaks through demonic strongholds, and even penetrates the barriers of hard human hearts. It does not need physical strength, human capabilities, or the right tools in order to work. God can answer our prayers at any time in any corner of the world.

Prayers are powerful because *they are undying.* True prayers are never lost. They are preserved forever in God's perfect memory. Long after we have forgotten what we prayed, God still remembers.

Even after death the prayers we prayed in life live on before God. He remembers and remains committed to respond to our uttered prayers in His own time and in His own way to the very end of the world (Revelation 8:3–5).

Our prayers are powerful because God is powerful—powerful to bless, powerful to transform, powerful to change things, powerful to meet any human need, at any time, in any place, in any way. And, you and I have the opportunity, through our prayers, to be part of what God in His power is doing. Amazing, don't you think?

Something to **Think** About

• Are there times when prayer is not powerful? Explain your answer.

• Why do you think God has decided to give believers the ability to move His hands through prayer? Why doesn't He just do what He wants to do?

• Is the power of prayer a power that can be abused? Why or why not?

• What God-dishonoring circumstance in the world today would you most like to see changed by means of powerful prayer? Pray about that circumstance and then thank God for His willingness to involve you and your prayers to bring about change.

Something to **Pray** About

• *Praise* God for the ability He has to answer any prayer, at any time, in any place.

- *Thank* God for the power He has put in your own hands and in the hands of all believers through prayer.
- If you have failed to use the prayer power that God has given you for Him, *confess* that to Him for the sin that it is.
- *Ask* God to make you a powerful intercessor.
- *Commit* yourself to using the prayer power God has given you.

Something to **Act** On

As you pray for specific persons try to remember three things about God:

1. God is omnipresent so He is with them.
2. God is omniscient so He knows what is best for them.
3. God is omnipotent so He is able to do what is best for them.

CHAPTER 11

God Answers Prayer in Different Ways

So Peter was kept in prison, but the church was earnestly praying to God for him. The night before Herod was to bring him to trial, Peter was sleeping between two soldiers, bound with two chains, and sentries stood guard at the entrance. Suddenly an angel of the Lord appeared and a light shone in the cell. He struck Peter on the side and woke him up. "Quick, get up!" he said, and the chains fell off Peter's wrists.

Peter came to himself and said, "Now I know without a doubt that the Lord sent his angel and rescued me from Herod's clutches."
—Acts 12:5–7, 11

At Caesarea there was a man named Cornelius, a centurion in what was known as the Italian Regiment. He and all his family were devout and God-fearing; he gave generously to those in need and prayed to God regularly. One day at about three in the afternoon he had a vision. He distinctly saw an angel of God, who came to him and said, "Cornelius!"

Cornelius stared at him in fear. "What is it, Lord?" he asked.

The angel answered, "Your prayers and gifts to the poor have come up as a memorial offering before God. Now send men to Joppa to bring back a man named Simon who is called Peter. He is staying with Simon the tanner, whose house is by the sea."

While Peter was still thinking about [his own] vision, the Spirit

said to him, "Simon, three men are looking for you. So get up and go

downstairs. Do not hesitate to go with them, for I have sent them."

—Acts 10:1–6, 19

Have you ever thought about all the different ways that God has at His disposal to answer prayer? He can work naturally or supernaturally. He can use people, angels, or natural forces. He even used a burning bush to get Moses' attention. Being eternal He can shape history and arrange circumstances over many years so that they converge in an answer that seems to us to come just in the nick of time. And, when He answers a prayer today, He knows what the consequences will be for all of life's tomorrows.

In answering prayer God the Father always begins by working with His Son, *Jesus Christ.* Christ is in charge of all earth operations. Paul said, "God placed all things under his feet and appointed him to be head over everything for the church" (Ephesians 1:22). "To be head over everything" means that He is responsible for answers to prayer. Jesus acknowledged as much when He said: "I will do whatever you ask in my name, so that the Son may being glory to the Father" (John 14:13). So, no matter what you are praying for, Jesus is the first responder. When you pray, Jesus acts.

When it comes to answering prayer, however, Christ never works alone. He always works through the *Spirit* to accomplish the Father's will. The Spirit, in cooperation with the Father and the Son, is also always involved in answering our prayers. Already in Old Testament times the Spirit was active in conveying God's gifts to people. When God had a message to deliver, it was the Spirit who prompted men and women to speak the word (2 Peter 1:21). When Moses needed help in leading Israel, God took some of the Spirit that was on him and placed it on seventy other prospective leaders (Numbers 11:16–17). When Jesus was preparing to leave He promised the disciples that He would ask the Father to send them another Counselor—one who would do for them everything that Christ had done (John 14:16–17). When they needed power, the Spirit would provide that (Luke 24:49). When they needed wisdom or revelation, the Spirit would give them that (Ephesians 1:17). When they prayed for filling, for fruit, for spiritual gifts, or for help in prayer it was the Spirit, sent by the Father and the Son, who delivered. When you pray the Spirit moves!

God also uses *angels* as His representatives in answering our prayers. While the Holy Spirit is normally the one who acts when the need is in the inner world of heart, soul, and mind; angels, directed by the Son and the Spirit, are typically the responders when help is needed in the natural world. They open prison doors (Acts 5:18), shut the mouths of lions (Daniel 6:22), protect from scorching fire (Daniel 3:25), and guard believers (Psalm 91:11). God's Word tells us that they are "ministering spirits sent to serve those who will inherit salvation" (Hebrews 1:14). Many times angels are sent in response to prayers. When Jerusalem was surrounded by the Assyrian army, King Hezekiah prayed and God sent an angel to strike a death blow to that great army (Isaiah 37:14, 36). While Peter was being held under guard in Herod's most secure prison, "the church was praying earnestly to God for him" (Acts 12:5). In response God sent an angel who effortlessly dealt with guards, shackles, and prison doors and set Peter free. As history comes to a close, it will once again be the prayers of the saints and the activities of angels that activate the final cataclysmic upheaval (Revelation 5:8, 8:4–5). When you pray God may just say to an angel, "Go and do it."

A fourth and common way that God answers prayers is through

persons. God loves to use persons in His kingdom projects. In response to the cries of the Hebrews in Egypt, God sent Moses. In response to Moses' "slow of speech" complaint, God sent Aaron. When Jesus saw that there was a plentiful harvest and too few workers, He said: "Ask the Lord of harvest, therefore, to send out workers into his harvest field" (Matthew 9:38). When it was time for the gospel to break out of its Jewish boundaries, God responded to the prayers of Cornelius and sent a person—Peter. Sometimes when we pray God sends a person—a person directed by Christ and empowered by the Spirit.

A fifth way that God answers prayer is through *forces of nature*, often forces that defy the normal laws of nature. When Israel was trapped between the armies of Egypt and the Red Sea, God heard the Israelites' cries of desperation and opened a path through the sea on dry land (Exodus 14:19–31). When Joshua needed extra time to complete a mission, he prayed and God made the sun stand still (Joshua 10:13). When Elijah asked for fire to fall on his water-soaked sacrifice on Mt. Carmel, God sent a fire that evaporated the sacrifice, the wood, the stones, the soil, and the water (1 Kings 18:38). There are no limits to what God can do in response to the prayers of His people. Sometimes when you pray God uses the forces of nature in surprising ways.

In fact God can use whatever means are necessary in any way He chooses. We can never standardize what He does or predict exactly how He will decide to respond. He may choose to answer our prayers by any one of the above means, or by any combination of them. Think about the combination of means the Lord used in bringing the gospel to the Gentiles. When He answered Cornelius's prayer He first sent an *angel* to give him directions, and then He gave Peter a *vision* in the sky to prepare him. That was followed by a word from the *Spirit,* convincing Peter to go. Finally, Peter himself became God's *human* answer as he went to preach the gospel to Cornelius and his waiting group in Caesarea (Acts 12:5–7, 11).

Thank God that we don't have to figure out *how* He's going to answer our prayers. We can leave that up to Him. But we do have to trust that He *will* answer, and that in His own time and in His own way. That He will do!

Something to **Think** About

• What are some of the most common ways that God seems to answer prayer today?

• Has God ever answered one of your intercessory prayers in a surprising or unexpected way? Explain.

• Has God ever used *you* to answer the intercessory prayers of someone else? Explain?

• In 2 Corinthians 4:18 Paul says, "So we fix our eyes not on what is seen, but on what is unseen." Would our prayers be different if we could always do that? Why or why not?

Something to **Pray** About

• *Praise* God for His ability to answer prayer in a variety of ways.
• *Thank* God for the ministering angels and the people that He sends to serve us.
• If you have given God few opportunities to act in response to prayer, *confess* that and seek His forgiveness.

- *Ask* God to help you trust that He will always answers your prayers in the best way.
- *Ask* God to send ministering angels to protect your loved ones from harm and from the powers of darkness.

Something to Act On

Try to formulate a prayer that might involve the following:

1. An *angel*—such as a prayer for a person in physical danger
2. A *person*—such as a prayer for a person to step in to meet a need
3. *Natural forces*—such as a prayer that requires an extraordinary healing

CHAPTER 12

Obedience Leads to Answers

Dear friends, if our hearts do not condemn us, we have confidence before God and receive from him anything we ask, because we obey his commands and do what pleases him. —1 John 3:21–22

Delight yourself in the LORD and he will give you the desires of your heart. Commit your way to the LORD; trust in him and he will do this: He will make your righteousness shine like the dawn, the justice of your cause like the noonday sun. —Psalm 37:4–6

Obedience is bottom line when it comes to getting answers to our intercessory prayers. The apostle John forged the link between answered prayer and obedience when he said: "If our hearts do not condemn us, we have confidence before God and *receive from him anything we ask*, because we *obey his commands* and do what pleases him" (emphasis added). James, though using different words, said essentially the same thing: "The prayer of a *righteous man* is powerful and effective" (James 5:16). The bottom line in both of these passages is simply this—to pray powerfully you must obey faithfully.

The truly obedient person not only understands *what* God wants prayed but *how* God wants life to be lived. Such a person has bought into God's plans and purposes. He or she is tracking with God, appreciating the wisdom of God's commands and living in accord with His ways. The obedience of such a person flows from a heart filled with love for the Father. It is a life-gift to God.

When we are sold out to God, committed to obeying His commands and doing what pleases Him, we will, as John says, "receive from him anything we ask." This promise is not simply a formula that works by some law of logic. It requires personal relational commitments: a commitment on our part to love and serve God, and a commitment on God's part to hear our prayers. It's a two-way love relationship in which each of the parties is determined to be a blessing to the other. Our commitment to obey is a commitment to a Person. God's commitment to answer prayer is a commitment to an obedient child. When our intercessory prayers come out of a heart filled with love and unswerving loyalty to Him, they will be prayers that God wants to answer.

If we listen to God and are committed to obeying Him, He listens to us and is committed to doing what we ask. This is not simply a matter of listening to God so that we can pray back to Him what He wants prayed. It is listening to what God has to say about all of life and living life in accord with what we hear. In other words, the power of prayer depends not just on right thinking but on right living. When our lives reflect the Word of God and our prayers are in accord with the will of God, then God will grant what we ask.

Imagine an employee who is totally loyal to his company. He has bought in to the company's vision and business practices. He sees the wisdom of the company's policies and tries to honor them in his way of working. He works hard and serves with distinction. He appreciates the owner and tries hard to do what's best for the company. If that owner is a wise and gracious person and this employee comes to him with a well-thought-out request for the good of the company, the employee will certainly receive a sympathetic hearing.

It is like that when we pray. When our will lines up with God's desires, He wills to give us what we ask. When we delight in His ways, He delights in our prayers. Was this not what David had in mind when he wrote, "Delight yourself in the LORD and he will give you the desires of your heart" (Psalm 37:4)? When we agree with Him, He chooses to agree with us and our requests.

Think for a moment of what it means to obey God's commands and do what pleases Him. Wouldn't it mean that we are committed to glorifying God in everything; seeking His kingdom above everything else; loving Him with all our heart, soul, and mind; worshiping Him in spirit and truth, and serving Him wholeheartedly, and believing in the name of His Son? It's not hard to imagine that believers, committed to such obedience, are going to pray prayers that are pleasing to God—prayers that God will happily answer with a yes. Or to turn that around, when believers are determined to do what pleases Him, then their prayers are not going to be filled with sinful, selfish, wrongly motivated requests. They will be prayers pleasing to God.

God's commands also cover our relationships with those around us: love one another, love your neighbor as yourself, bear one another's burdens, love your enemies, be My witnesses, be kind and compassionate to one another, forgive one another, and pray for one another. If these commands, and many more like them, are lodged in our hearts and affect the way we relate to and pray for others, then God will have ample reason to hear and answer our prayers. Intercessory prayers that reflect our obedience to these relationship commands will be "powerful and effective."

Two questions, however, remain. The first question is: can we actually meet the requirement of obeying His commands and doing what pleases Him? The answer is no if we are trying to do it in our own strength. But the answer is yes if we are acting in Christ's strength. John said, "Those who obey his commands live in him, and he in them" (1 John 3:24). It is when we live in Him and He lives in us that we have the strength to obey His commands. When Christ abides in us we have His love, His power, His mind, His grace, and His life in us. Christ's supreme desire was to live in accord with the Father's will. When Christ lives in us, that same desire dominates our lives. Having that desire we are able to meet the conditions necessary in order to claim the promise of answered prayer.

The second question is: do we have to live lives of sinless perfection in order to claim this prayer promise? Again, I think the answer is no. If that were true no one could claim the promise. We are not able to live sinless lives. John reminds us that "If we claim to be without sin, we deceive ourselves and the truth is not in us" (1 John 1:8). If, however, we are trying to please God in all we do, truly hate sin, and readily repent of any sins that we become aware of, then this prayer promise is for us. If, however, we disobey with calloused hearts, relish sin, and remain unrepentant, then we should not expect God to hear and answer our prayers. It is not sinless perfection that God looks for, but an attitude toward sin that is like His.

If you want to pray well, then learn how to obey well. No man can really pray well who is not intent on obeying God's commands and pleasing Him. Obedience produces powerful and effective prayers. Disobedience induces weak and ineffective prayers. You make the choice. You can and you must!

Something to **Think** About

- Why would the Lord be inclined to give us "the desires of our hearts" if we are delighting in Him?

• Will God be blessed and glorified if He gives you what you are currently asking Him in behalf of others? Try to verbalize the "how" in your answer.

• If sin hinders prayer and both believers and unbelievers sin, why would God be inclined to answer the prayers of believers and not the prayers of unbelievers?

Something to **Pray** About

• *Praise* God for His wisdom in giving us rules for living that, if followed, will bring us great blessing.
• *Thank* God for His readiness to make the prayers of the righteous "powerful and effective."
• *Ask* God for the help you need to obey His commands and do what pleases Him.
• If you have been expecting God to answer your prayers while you were not living in accord with His will, *confess* that to Him and *recommit* yourself to wholehearted obedience.

Something to **Act** On

Tell God how committed you are to obey His commands and do what pleases Him. Ask Him for the wisdom to know and the strength to do what pleases Him. Then, remind yourself of His promise to those who obey, and carry His Spirit-given confidence into your prayer times.

CHAPTER 13

Praying by "the Book"

If you remain in me and my words remain in you, ask whatever you wish, and it will be given you. —John 15:7

Consequently, faith comes from hearing the message, and the message is heard through the word of Christ. —Romans 10:17

"The Book" I have in mind is the Bible, the Word of God. Knowing the Bible well is key to effective prayer. Here's why! To pray well we have to know His will. To know His will we have to hear Him speak. To hear Him speak we have to read the Word. The Bible is not the only way we hear God today, but it is the primary way. From the Bible we come to know God's mind, His heart, and His purposes; it's a "knowing" that informs our prayers. This is true for intercessory prayer as well as all other kinds of prayer.

We have touched on the theme of hearing God in previous chapters. In chapter 6, "The Listening Side of Intercession," we observed how Elijah and Daniel first heard God's Word and then prayed for Him to do what He had announced He would do. In chapter 8, "Praying Kingdom Prayers," we said that believers should pray for the purposes of God as clearly revealed in the Word: His glory, His kingdom, His will, the spread of the gospel, His church, and the return of Christ. In this chapter we'll discover how God's will, revealed in the scriptures, can and should shape our prayers for others. Allowing the scriptures to shape our intercessory prayers will make them more effective. God's Word will help us, first of all, to *keep our eyes fixed on the God* who hears and answers prayer. Prayer works because God works. He is actively at work in the world in response to our prayers. It is easy to get our prayer focus on the words we pray, the length of our prayers, or the posture in which we pray and to think that these are what make prayer effective. The scriptures, however, always point us back to God as the reason that prayer is effective. In a crisis situation, Israel's king Jehoshaphat prayed, "O our God . . . we have no power to face this vast army. . . . We do not know what to do, but our eyes are upon you" (2 Chronicles 20:12). Like Jehoshaphat we need to fix our eyes on God, with an awareness of our deficiencies and His sufficiency.

Praying by "the Book" helps us to *pray what God wants prayed.* The scriptures help us see as God sees, think as He thinks, and feel as He feels. As God's perspective filters into our hearts, we are able to see circumstances as He sees them and pray into them with His heart. Self-generated prayers fabricated within our own sin-prone hearts will be nothing but meager. But, fed by scripture and guided by the Holy Spirit, our hearts will work to align our prayers with His purposes. Such prayers, formed out of the scriptures, will be powerful and effective. Jesus' promise to give His disciples whatever they wished was based not only on their remaining in Him, but on His words remaining in them (John 15:7).

Praying the scriptures will *enrich the content of our prayers.* God is an expert in all areas of human experience. By drawing on His Word we can learn how to pray about a variety of human situations. The prayers of the embattled church of Jerusalem, reported in early Acts, can teach us how to pray in the face of threats and persecution.

Paul's well-focused prayers for believers in the churches he planted will inform our prayers for other believers we know. The Psalms, most of which are prayers, are particularly helpful. Eugene Peterson has reminded us that "everything a person can possibly feel, experience or say is brought to expression in the Psalms."[1] All that we learn about the main themes of life from scripture—sin, salvation, service, faith, hope, love, peace, wisdom, grace, and so on—will help us to pray meaningfully into human situations.

Rooting our prayers in scripture will tend to *rouse the compassions of God in our hearts*. The feelings that we bring to our prayers are often inaccurate. If we know God's will and God's Word well, we are much more likely to be able to feel what He feels and to pray with His love and compassion. Matthew tells us of Jesus that "when he saw the crowds, he had compassion on them, because they were harassed and helpless, like sheep without a shepherd" (Matthew 9:36). Jesus' compassion for the crowds soon led Him to urge the disciples to pray for harvest workers. If the compassion of Christ is roused within us, our prayers will certainly be more heartfelt.

Praying scripture will *strengthen the faith* that we bring to our prayers. Paul asserted that "faith comes from hearing the message, and the message is heard through the word of Christ" (Romans 10:17). The more certain we are of what God wants to do in the lives of those for whom we pray, the more faith we will bring to that prayer of intercession. When, for example, I pray for my children and grandchildren that their "love may abound more and more in knowledge and depth of insight," so that they "may be able to discern what is best and may be pure and blameless until the day of Christ, filled with the fruit of righteousness" (Philippians 1:9–11), I know that God hears and answers that prayer. I know it because I know that is what God wants to do. My faith in God's response comes from hearing the Word and transposing it into a prayer of intercession.

Following are some how-to tips when interceding by "the Book":

Ask the Holy Spirit to *direct you* to persons or situations for which He would like you to pray "Book" prayers. As God directs you He will be revealing something of His plans and purposes for these persons or situations.

With the Spirit's help try to *identify the real spiritual need* that should be addressed when you are praying for someone else. This will often mean getting beyond the presenting problem to an issue that lies beneath the surface. The real need might be a sin that needs to be confessed, a discipline that needs to be developed, a promise that needs to be claimed, or a bondage that needs to be broken.

Pray *for God and for His purposes* in that person's life or in that situation. In other words, be God-focused rather than need-focused in your prayers. Ask the question, "What would bring God glory in this situation, what would advance His kingdom, what would accomplish His will?"

Ask God to *lead you to a scripture passage* that applies to the person or situation you are praying about. Try to find and make use of scripture prayers or episodes that correspond to that situation. Ask the question, "Are there ways that persons in the biblical times prayed about such concerns?"

Praying the scripture for others means asking God to do for them what He really wants to. You will know what He wants to do if you find it in the Bible. If, for example, you pray that an unhappy friend will be able to "rejoice in the Lord always," you are praying Philippians 4:4. If you pray that a fellow believer will know how much they are worth to the Father, you might be praying Matthew 10:31: "Don't be afraid; you are worth more than many sparrows." If you pray that an immature Christian you know will "grow in the grace and knowledge of our Lord and Savior Jesus Christ," you are praying by "the Book" (2 Peter 3:18). You can multiply these simple examples by hundreds. It's as simple as that.

Something to **Think** About

- What difference will it make if your intercessory prayers are God-focused rather than need-focused? Try to think of a specific example.

- What could you do to sense the thoughts and feelings of Christ (such as His love, wisdom, compassion, joy, patience, or anger) when you are praying about a situation?

- Why would praying scripture tend to increase our faith?

Something to **Pray** About

- *Thank* God for the scriptures and the help they give us to pray effectively.
- If your intercessory prayers have been primarily pleas for help without much thought of God's purposes, *deal* with that before God.
- *Promise* God that you are going to learn to pray by "the Book," and then follow through.
- *Ask* God to help you become scripture oriented when you pray for others.

Something to **Act** On

Try out each of the four how-to suggestions above. Begin to use regularly the ones that work best for you.

CHAPTER 14

Praying for Family and Friends

People were bringing little children to Jesus to have him touch them, but the disciples rebuked them. When Jesus saw this, he was indignant. He said to them, "Let the little children come to me, and do not hinder them, for the kingdom of God belongs to such as these. I tell you the truth, anyone who will not receive the kingdom of God like a little child will never enter it." And he took the children in his arms, put his hands on them and blessed them. —Mark 10:13–16

"Simon, Simon, Satan has asked to sift you as wheat. But I have prayed for you, Simon, that your faith may not fail. And when you have turned back, strengthen your brothers." —Luke 22:31–32

Our first line of responsibility in intercessory prayer is for those who are relationally closest to us—our circle of family and friends. God has put them near us so that we can be His channels of love to them and release His power and grace into their lives through prayer. Being close to them we know their needs and know what to pray. We are also positioned to be God's instruments in answering the prayers we pray for them. And we will be among the first to see God's answers and to give Him thanks.

Jesus is our most important example of one who prayed for those relationally near Him. He prayed a blessing on the little children who were brought to Him. He prayed for Peter so that his faith would not fail. A few hours before His death, Jesus prayed that the Father would protect and sanctify His disciples and give them a spirit of unity. Paul also prayed for those whom he loved and cared about. To his "dear son" Timothy, he wrote, "Night and day I constantly remember you in my prayers" (2 Timothy 1:3). To Philemon, another friend and fellow worker, Paul wrote, "I always thank my God as I remember you in my prayers. . . . I pray that you may be active in sharing your faith" (Philemon 4, 6). And to the end of his days, Paul prayed passionately and faithfully for the new converts in the churches that he planted—converts whom he referred to as his brothers loved by God.

In this chapter we will look at eight biblical reasons why we should intercede for our family and friends and what we can expect to gain from praying. First, we can *bring family members to Jesus*. We can do what parents did when Jesus was physically on earth. They brought their little children to Jesus to have Him touch them. Mark reports that Jesus "took the children in his arms, put his hands on them and blessed them." Jesus is just as willing and just as able to bless today. It is His nature to want to bless. Try to imagine Him reaching down to spiritually lay His hands on and bless the family members that you bring to Him in prayer.

Second, we can *shore up their faith*. That's what Jesus did for Simon Peter. Even before Peter was "sifted" by Satan, Jesus prayed that his faith would not fail. Peter did deny his Lord in the hours that followed, but, thanks to Jesus' prayer, it was only a temporary failure. Peter's faith held and he rebounded to become the "rock" Jesus had called him to be. Faith to stay a God-given course is clearly among the foremost things that we should ask for family members and friends. John emphasized that faith is "the victory that has overcome the world" (1 John 5:4). Paul said that faith was the shield "with which you can extinguish all the flaming arrows of the evil one" (Ephesians 6:16). We can be sure that spiritual forces of evil will come against our family members and friends. We can also be sure that prayer will shore up their faith.

Third, we can *claim the promise of the Holy Spirit for our children.* After Peter had urged his hearers on the day of Pentecost to repent and be baptized, he promised that they would receive the gift of the Holy Spirit. He went on to say that the gift was for them *and their children* (Acts 2:38–39). God wants the children of believing parents to have the Holy Spirit. That's why He made the promise. Paul even calls children of true believers "holy" (1 Corinthians 7:14). Promises, of course, need to be claimed. When children come of age they have to claim God's promises for themselves. However, the promise-claiming prayers of parents and grandparents undergird the choices that children make when they come of age. There's no more important prayer for us to pray for our children than that they will have the Holy Spirit.

Fourth, our prayers can *release material blessings* into the lives of family and friends. In the Lord's Prayer Jesus teaches us to pray, "Give us today our daily bread" (Matthew 6:11). The "bread" for which we pray includes all our physical and material needs. The pronoun "us" is a strong reminder to pray for the material well-being of others as well as for ourselves. We can boldly ask the Father for the material blessings that others need, as well as spiritual blessings. As we pray for *our* daily bread, it's our family and friends that come to mind first.

Fifth, we can pray for *physical protection.* In God's way of working, prayer is a key factor in physical protection. When Peter was imprisoned and about to be executed, the church earnestly prayed to God for him. In response to their prayers, God protected Peter's life by arranging for a dramatic escape. In the face of a hurricane, Paul prayed for those on board the ship with him. God heard his prayer, spared his live, and graciously gave him the lives of all who sailed with him (Acts 27:24). A psalmist reminds us of God's power to provide physical protection when he writes: "He will command his angels concerning you to guard you in all your ways; they will lift you up in their hands, so that you will not strike your foot against a stone" (Psalm 91:11–12). You can put a hedge of protection around your families and friends by means of prayer.

Sixth, we can pray for *spiritual protection* for those we love and care for. A Canaanite woman came to Jesus, pleading for her daughter to be delivered from demon possession. Though Jesus tested her faith by putting her off at first, she boldly persisted in her pleas and even argued with His reasons for declining her request. Jesus ended up commending her faith and healing her daughter. Her persistent prayers provided spiritual deliverance for her demonized daughter. The Son of God, who appeared "to destroy the devil's work" (1 John 3:8), is still in the business of destroying the devil's work. He is delighted to hear our prayers for the spiritual protection of those in our immediate spheres of influence, and is eager to deliver them from evil. The evil one is still active. Our prayers for spiritual protection are still needed.

Seventh, our prayers can even *win a reversal of judgment*. More than once Moses' intercessory prayers for Israel brought about a reversal of God's judgment. When the Israelites were about to enter the Promised Land, Moses reminded them that the Lord "was angry enough with you to destroy you. But again the LORD listened to me" (Deuteronomy 9:19). The psalmist summarizes Moses' standing-in-the-gap work by saying: "So he [God] said he would destroy them—had not Moses, his chosen one, stood in the breach before him to keep his wrath from destroying them" (Psalm 106:23). God, who is the same yesterday, today, and forever, is willing to listen when we seek His mercy for those who have offended Him.

Finally, we can *model intercessory prayer* for our family members. The disciples heard Jesus' prayers of intercession. They sensed the compassion and faith with which He prayed. They saw the answers to His prayers. They learned firsthand that God is faithful in hearing and answering prayer and, as a result, they became intercessors. Jesus modeled what He taught. We can do the same thing for our family members and friends.

Your prayers can make a huge difference in the lives of your family and friends. Are you ready to step into the gap and be God's appointed intercessor for those in your sphere of influence? Isn't that where God wants you?

Something to **Think** About

- How does God want you to intercede for your family members and friends? Is there one or more of the eight biblical reasons above that you should focus on?

- Do you think that Jesus is as eager to bless children today as He was to bless the children brought to Him during His days on earth? What are the implications of your answer for you, if you are a parent or grandparent?

- Why is a shored-up faith so important? Explain.

• Many of the intercessors described above were bold. What does it mean to be bold in intercession?

Something to **Pray** About

• *Praise* Jesus as the ultimate intercessor who provides the perfect model for intercession.
• *Thank* God that you are able to bless the lives of those in your sphere of influence through prayer.
• If you have sinned against your family and/or friends by failing to pray for them, *confess* that to the Lord.
• *Ask* God to help you intercede faithfully and boldly for family and friends.
• *Commit* to intercede faithfully for family members and friends.

Something to **Act** On

Review the eight biblical reasons to pray for family and friends. Ask the Holy Spirit to alert you to the greatest needs in the lives of those around you. Focus your prayers on those areas of need.

CHAPTER 15

Praying for Spiritual Growth

For this reason I kneel before the Father, . . . I pray that out of his glorious riches he may strengthen you with power through his Spirit in your inner being, so that Christ may dwell in your hearts through faith. And I pray that you, being rooted and established in love, may have power, together with all the saints, to grasp how wide and long and high and deep is the love of Christ, and to know this love that surpasses knowledge—that you may be filled to the measure of all the fullness of God.
—Ephesians 3:14, 16–19

And this is my prayer: that your love may abound more and more in knowledge and depth of insight, so that you may be able to discern what is best and may be pure and blameless until the day of Christ, filled with the fruit of righteousness that comes through Jesus Christ—to the glory and praise of God. —Philippians 1:9–11

God was eager to see the new Christians in the early church grow spiritually. So was His servant Paul. God and Paul came together to make it happen. Paul interceded for the spiritual growth of the new believers, and God answered. As a result the early Christians grew spiritually in a way they would never have grown without Paul's asking and God's giving.

Paul was an amazing intercessor. I don't think any person ever prayed more faithfully and fervently for the spiritual growth of believers than Paul. His whole life and ministry was characterized by intercessory prayer. He taught prayer. he urged prayer, but more than anything else he prayed. Over and over again in his letters we hear him saying things such as "[I] have not stopped praying for you" (Colossians 1:9) and "I constantly remember you in my prayers" (2 Timothy 1:3) and "night and day we pray most earnestly" (1 Thessalonians 3:10).

Paul's prayers were not, however, simply a way to get God to solve personal problems or meet felt needs. The heartfelt desire of Paul was to see believers grow spiritually. Of the twenty-three prayer items in Paul's reported prayers, not one has to do with personal felt needs. All of them are prayers for the spiritual health and well-being of the new Christians that he loves.

 A careful look at the prayers of Paul reveals at least *five major themes.* His first theme has to do with *spiritual empowerment.* He prayed that the Ephesian Christians would be *strengthened with power* through God's Spirit in their inner being, so that Christ would dwell in their hearts through faith (Ephesians 3:16–17). Then he went on to assure them that God would do more than all they could ask or imagine "according to his *power* that is at work within us" (Ephesians 3:20, emphasis added). For the Colossians, he prayed that they would be "*strengthened with all power* according to his glorious *might*" (Colossians 1:11, emphasis added). He prayed that God would *strengthen* the hearts of the Thessalonians so that they could "be blameless and holy" (1 Thessalonians 3:13). Later he prayed that God would encourage their hearts and *strengthen* them "in every good deed and word" (2 Thessalonians 2:17). Paul knew that to grow spiritually they would need a spiritual power that could only be released through prayer.

2 Second, Paul prayed for _overflowing love_. He asked God to help the Ephesians be "rooted and established in _love_" and able "to grasp how wide and long and high and deep is the _love of Christ_, and to know this _love_ that surpasses knowledge" (Ephesians 3:17–19, emphasis added). For the Thessalonians, he prayed, "May the Lord make your _love_ increase and overflow for each other and for everyone else" (1 Thessalonians 3:12, emphasis added). Later he added: "May the Lord direct your hearts into _God's love_" (2 Thessalonians 3:5, emphasis added). He asked for the Philippians that their _love_ would "abound more and more in knowledge and depth of insight" (Philippians 1:9). Paul, overflowing in love himself, asks God to give His children that same love.

3 Third, Paul prayed for _wisdom_ and the closely related virtues of knowledge, understanding, spiritual enlightenment, and depth of insight. Paul prayed that the Ephesians would be given the _Spirit of wisdom and revelation_ so that they might know God better and that the eyes of their hearts would be _enlightened_ (Ephesians 1:17–18). He asked God to fill the Colossians with the knowledge of His will "through all spiritual _wisdom and understanding_" (Colossians 1:9–10, emphasis added). He interceded for _knowledge and depth of insight_ for the Philippians so that they would be "able to _discern_ what was best" (Philippians 1:9–10, emphasis added). Paul, out of the wisdom God gave to him, prayed that others might have wisdom.

4 Fourth, Paul prayed for _holiness_. He began by asking that the Thessalonians would be "_blameless and holy_ in the presence of our God and Father" (1 Thessalonians 3:13, emphasis added) and then ended his letter to them, saying: "May God himself, the God of peace, _sanctify_ you [make you holy] through and through. May your whole _spirit, soul and body be kept blameless_ at the coming of our Lord Jesus Christ" (1 Thessalonians 5:23, emphasis added). He asked God

to make the Philippians *"pure and blameless* until the day of Christ" (Philippians 1:10, emphasis added). Paul was big on holiness and prayed for it vigorously for those whom he loved.

⑤   Fifth, Paul prayed for *spiritual fruitfulness*. He prayed that the Philippians would be "filled with the *fruit of righteousness* that comes through Jesus Christ" (Philippians 1:11, emphasis added). He was convinced that the Colossians, in response to his asking, would be *"bearing fruit* in every good work" (Colossians 1:10, emphasis added). He blessed the Romans with "*joy* and *peace*" so that they "may overflow with *hope* by the power of the Holy Spirit" (Romans 15:13, emphasis added). In Paul's view there would be no spiritual fruitfulness without fervent prevailing prayer.

What a great way this is to pray for those we love and care about. What's so great about it is that we know that God is both willing and able to give these kinds of blessings to His children! He is almighty! Empowering believers is no problem for Him. He is love! For Him to cause His children to overflow in love is a breeze. He is an all-wise Father. It doesn't surprise us that He would delight to give wisdom, insight, and enlightenment to His children. And, of course, being holy Himself, God wants us to be holy (1 Peter 1:16) and will do what it takes to accomplish that. And when we pray for fruitfulness, He says, no problem: all spiritual fruit is simply the fruit of the Spirit (Galatians 5:22–23). Touched by the fervent prayers of faithful intercessors, God does not hold back.

If God is both willing and able to provide these blessings, then why doesn't He just give them to us? He surely knows that we need them! The answer is because God wants to be asked for what He wants to give. That is the way He has chosen to work. Asking keeps us coming back to Him. Continually coming to God enhances our relationship with Him. An enhanced, intimate relationship with

God means that we understand His heart and will better—and that leads to more effective intercession. Imagine what would happen if the billions of Christians in the world today were to pray faithfully and fervently for spiritual power, overflowing love, wisdom, holiness, and fruitfulness for themselves and for others. The results would be staggering. But that is surely what God intends, and that is why He appointed Paul to model for us the value of interceding for spiritual growth; and then He reminds us no less than seven times in the Bible to imitate Paul (see 1 Corinthians 4:16, 11:1).

Do you want to be a powerful intercessor? You can be! The power in prayer is not in you. All the power in prayer is God's power released through our prayers. And God is as powerful today as He ever was. Why not start today, interceding for spiritual growth for your family and friends. Then, expand your prayers to cover your local church. Finally, move beyond that to pray for spiritual growth in all believers. That kind of praying just might spark a revival!

Something to **Think** About

- How does Paul's pattern of interceding compare with the kinds of intercession you hear today?

- What do you think would happen in a believer's life if he or she received steady doses of power, love, wisdom, holiness, and fruitfulness from God because he or she was being prayed for?

- Could your prayers be as powerful as Paul's prayers were? Why or why not?

Something to **Pray** About

- *Praise* God whose might, wisdom, love, holiness, and fruit-bearing ability undergirds all that He does for us.
- *Thank* God for His ability and His willingness to give you power, wisdom, love, holiness, and fruitfulness.
- If you have failed to pray for the spiritual growth of family members and fellow believers, *confess* that to God and claim His forgiving grace before you go on.
- *Ask* God for power, wisdom, love, holiness, and spiritual fruitfulness for yourself.
- Make a *commitment* before God to intercede for the spiritual growth of those in your circle of influence.

Something to **Act** On

Enlarge your understanding of Paul's five spiritual growth prayer themes from the following scripture passages:

Power: 2 Peter 1:3–4

Love: Deuteronomy 6:4–9

Wisdom: James 3:17; Proverbs 3:13–14

Holiness: 2 Corinthians 7:1

Fruit-bearing: Galatians 5:22–23

Pray these five spiritual blessings into the lives of those around you. Trust that God is willing and able to answer your prayers for them in His own time and way.

CHAPTER 16

Praying Your Friends to Christ

*The god of this age has blinded the minds of unbelievers, so that they
cannot see the light of the gospel of the glory of Christ, who is the image
of God. . . . For God, who said, "Let light shine out of darkness,"
made his light shine in our hearts to give us the light of the knowledge of
the glory of God in the face of Christ.* —2 Corinthians 4:4, 6

*I urge, then, first of all, that requests, prayers, intercession and thanks-
giving be made for everyone. . . . This is good, and pleases God our
Savior, who wants all people to be saved and to come to a knowledge of
the truth. For there is one God and one mediator between God and human beings, Christ Jesus, himself human, who gave himself as a ransom
for all people.* —1 Timothy 2:1, 3–6, TNIV

One of the most important assignments believers have is to pray
family and friends to Christ. Jesus interceded for future converts when He said to the Father, "I pray also for those who will
believe in me through their [disciples'] message" (John 17:20). Paul
interceded for the salvation of fellow Jews with heartfelt prayer:
"Brothers and sisters, my heart's desire and prayer to God for the
Israelites is that they may be saved" (Romans 10:1, TNIV). In a
letter to Timothy, Paul urged that "requests, prayers, intercession

and thanksgiving be made for everyone." Such praying, said Paul, "pleases God our Savior, who wants all people to be saved and to come to a knowledge of the truth." The New Testament picture is certainly clear. Prayer precedes conversion.

To pray effectively for unconverted persons, we need to see them as God sees them. The Bible makes it plain that God has a heart for unsaved persons. He does not want anyone to perish, but wants "everyone to come to repentance" (2 Peter 3:9). He is willing to grant them "repentance leading . . . to a knowledge of the truth . . . and escape from the trap of the devil" (2 Timothy 2:25–26). He sent His Son "to seek and to save what was lost" (Luke 19:10). And His Son, who came "to save the world" (John 3:17), commissioned others "to open their eyes and turn them from darkness to light, and from the power of Satan to God, so that they may receive forgiveness of sins" (Acts 26:18). Our Father God, like the father in Jesus' story of the prodigal son, yearns for and watches for His prodigal sons and daughters to come home. He wants to save! He is able to save! He moves in the lives of people when we pray.

Satan, on the other hand, does everything in his power to keep unsaved persons in his grip. Jesus exposed Satan as the "strong man" who tries to keep his possessions "safe" by being "fully armed" as "he guards his own house" (Luke 11:21). This same evil one seeks to hinder their salvation by blinding their eyes "so that they cannot see the light of the gospel of the glory of Christ" (2 Corinthians 4:4), and snatches away the seed of the gospel message sown in their hearts (Matthew 13:19). Those who reject the gospel remain in "the trap of the devil, who has taken them captive to do his will" (2 Timothy 2:26).

Scripture gives us important insights on **what to pray** for those who don't know Christ.

Pray that *the Father will draw* unsaved persons to Himself. Jesus said, "No one can come to me unless the Father who sent me draws him" (John 6:44). The unsaved persons for whom you pray will not go to Christ out of their own volition. They can't. But the Father who can draw them delights to do so in response to our asking.

Pray that *they will come to repentance.* The Lord wants unsaved persons to come to repentance and to be saved (2 Peter 3:9). And He wants us to pray for that. God will welcome their repentance so that He can purge out what hinders their salvation and give them new life.

Pray that *they will hear and understand the gospel.* They have to hear. Paul was making this point when he asked, "How can they believe in the one of whom they have not heard?" (Romans 10:14). And they have to understand. Jesus warned that Satan would snatch the seed of the gospel away from those who don't understand (Matthew 13:19).

Pray that *their minds will be opened.* Satan tries to blind the minds of unbelievers, "so that they cannot see the light of the gospel of the glory of Christ" (2 Corinthians 4:4). God wants to open their minds so they will see the "light." Opening human minds is God's business. But moving God's Spirit to do so is prayer business.

Pray that *they will be freed from Satan's bondage.* The devil is a defeated enemy. He is the "strong man" who is bound by Jesus (Luke 11:21). He is the "power" disarmed by Jesus (Colossians 2:14). The devil can deal with any force that we humans can bring against him, but he cannot deal with the hands of almighty God moved through our prayers. Ask God to thwart Satan's plans by unbinding and unblinding the persons for whom you pray, so that "they will come to their senses and escape from the trap of the devil" (2 Timothy 2:26).

Scripture also gives some clues on **how to pray** for those who don't know Christ.

Pray with a *compassionate concern* that reflects the Father's heart. Intercession is not a matter of dispassionately presenting our thoughts and words to God. God not only hears our prayers, He weighs them—weighs the burden in our hearts.

Pray with *faith*. Believe that the Lord is willing. He "wants all people to be saved" and is pleased with the prayers that make this happen (1 Timothy 2:4, TNIV). Believe that He is able: "With God all things are possible" (Matthew 19:26).

Pray with *boldness*. In Jesus' story of the midnight visitor, the host, who pleads with a neighbor for bread to serve his friend, knocks persistently and boldly. Jesus commends his boldness and says, "Because of the man's boldness he will get up and give him as much as he needs" (Luke 11:5–8). Pray boldly for persons who do not know Jesus. God will be pleased.

Be willing to invest time, *plenty of time*. Intercession is work and all work takes time. Effective intercessors are always on watch for the Lord (see Isaiah 62:6–7).

Finally, pray *continuously*. Never give up! God's timing in not our timing. He wants "all people to be saved and to come to a knowledge of the truth" (1 Timothy 2:4). That includes unsaved family, friends, and neighbors for whom you are praying.

As God begins to change the hearts and lives of unsaved persons you are praying for, make yourself available to those persons if that is at all possible. Tell the Lord you are willing to be used in their lives. Reach out to them in loving, caring ways. And, once a person receives Christ, don't stop praying. Thank God for your new brother or sister in Christ and then double your prayer efforts for them, knowing that Satan will double his efforts to pull them back into his web of doubts, deceits, and sinful entanglements. Persist in prayer until they are well established in the faith.

Something to **Think** About

- Try to imagine a loved one you are praying for chained and hand-cuffed by Satan, blind to the good news of Jesus Christ, and held captive in the devil's grip. How does that make Jesus feel? How does that make you feel?

- Next, imagine that Jesus and you are with that same loved one. Jesus wants to unchain them, open their eyes to the "light," and set them free from the devil's prison. What does Jesus want *you* to do in this situation?

- Which of the five insights on *what to pray* for unconverted persons do you most need to work on? How do you plan to do that?

- Which of the five clues on *how to pray* for unconverted persons do you most need to work on? How are you going to do that?

Something to **Pray** About

- *Praise* the Lord as a God of salvation.
- *Thank* God for hearing and answering the "conversion" prayers that others prayed for you.
- If you have sinned against an unsaved person you know by failing to pray for them in the way God wants you too, *confess* that and find His forgiveness.
- *Ask* God for help to intercede for unconverted persons you know.

Something to **Act** On

Identify the suggestions in this chapter that fit your prayer life. Begin to implement them. If praying for those who don't know Christ is new for you, start by focusing on one person. As you grow stronger in prayer ask God for additional assignments.

CHAPTER 17

Praying for Spiritual Leaders

I urge you, brothers, by our Lord Jesus Christ and by the love of the Spirit, to join me in my struggle by praying to God for me. Pray that I may be rescued from the unbelievers in Judea and that my service in Jerusalem may be acceptable to the saints there, so that by God's will I may come to you with joy and together with you be refreshed.

—Romans 15:30–32

On him we have set our hope that he will continue to deliver us, as you help us by your prayers. Then many will give thanks on our behalf for the gracious favor granted to us in answer to the prayers of many.

—2 Corinthians 1:10–11

Spiritual leaders need prayer support. The apostle Paul surely thought he needed the prayer support of his friends. It's is one of the main features of his letters. Five times he asks for prayer.* Twice he reports the results of other's prayers for him.** Many spiritual leaders today are not as aware as Paul was of their need for prayer support. Yet, they need it as much as he did, possibly even more.

*(Romans 15:30–32; Ephesians 6:19–20; Colossians 4:3–4; 1 Thessalonians 5:25; 2 Thessalonians 3:1–2)
**(2 Corinthians 1:10–11; Philippians 1:19)

Spiritual leaders need prayer because they *will be judged more strictly* than other Christians. James cautions his readers: "Not many of you should presume to be teachers . . . because you know that we who teach will be judged more strictly" (James 3:1). God has always chosen to accomplish His purposes through men and women whom He chooses and calls into leadership roles. Their responsibilities are daunting and the stakes are high. Those entrusted with God's work cannot accomplish God's purposes by means of unaided human strength. Without the support of intercessory prayer they are bound to fail.

Spiritual leaders have *more than average influence.* That's why Satan targets them as he does. He knows that to discredit a spiritual leader is to discredit Christ and His church—at least temporarily. If Satan can bring down a person of influence, that's a huge "win" for his side. That's why he came after Jesus and Paul and Jesus' twelve disciples so tenaciously. We have a saying: "The bigger they are, the harder they fall." Satan's version of that is: "The bigger they are, the greater my gain when they fall."

Spiritual leaders today are *under attack from an enemy* who is intent on demoralizing and defaming them. A recent Focus on the Family survey uncovered the fact that 33 percent of pastors felt lonely, discouraged, or exhausted from ministry; and 21 percent had sought help for depression. Another survey done by *Christianity Today* revealed that 37 percent of pastors struggle with cyber porn. Accord to George Barna's research, more than 1,500 pastors are leaving the ministry every month in the United States due to burnout, moral indiscretion, or forced resignation. Dire statistics like these underscore the great need today for all believers to lift up their pastors and other spiritual leaders in faithful, fervent intercessory prayer.

Spiritual leaders are *experiencing pain and strain.* In Romans 15,

Paul pleads for fellow Christians to "join me in my struggle." The word he uses for "struggle" literally means, "strive together with." Our English word "agony" comes from the same root. In other words, the struggle Paul has in mind involves pain and strain to the point of agony. If you really want to be an effective intercessor, ask God to reveal to you the pain and strain of the spiritual leaders you pray for so that, as you intercede, you are able to feel their pain and step into it with them. You will be joining the ranks of suffering servants who serve the Suffering Servant.

Pray for *spiritual protection*. It seems that spiritual protection was on the top of Paul's list of personal prayer requests. He asks the Romans to pray that he might "be rescued from the unbelievers in Judea" (Romans 15:31). He wants the Thessalonians to pray "that we may be delivered from wicked and evil men" (2 Thessalonians 3:2). Based on the prayers of the Corinthians he expects that God "will continue to deliver us" (2 Corinthians 1:10); and he reports to the Philippians that through their prayers and the help of the Spirit "what has happened to me will turn out for my deliverance" (Philippians 1:19). The spiritual leaders you know may not ask for prayer protection as Paul did, but they need it more than ever today, whether or not they ask. Your prayers can put a hedge of protection around spiritual leaders and their families and ward off the devil and his predators.

Pray for *fruitful ministry*. Fruitful ministry was also high on Paul's prayer list. He urged the Romans to pray that his "service in Jerusalem may be acceptable to the saints there" (Romans 15:31). He asked the Ephesians to pray that "whenever I open my mouth, words may be given me so that I will fearlessly make known the mystery of the gospel" (Ephesians 6:19). He wanted the Colossians to pray that God would "open a door for our message, so that we may proclaim the mystery of Christ" (Colossians 4:3), and he requested that the Thessalonians pray "that the message of the Lord may spread rapidly and be honored" (2 Thessalonians 3:1). Paul was clearly convinced that the success of his ministry depended on prayer. And it did! Those early Christians did pray. And with Paul taking the lead, the gospel spread throughout the Roman Empire like a California wildfire. Prayer is key to fruitful ministry and the spread of the gospel.

Pray for personal *joy and refreshment.* Among the things Paul longed for and asked the Roman Christians to pray for was that he would be able to come to them "with joy" and together with them "be refreshed" (Romans 15:32). Weariness and discouragement are some of Satan's strongest weapons. A report from Shepherd's Ministries noted that 78,000 pastors had left the ministry in a recent year. You can be sure that most of those left feeling beaten down and discouraged. Despite all that he endured (see 2 Corinthians 11:24–28) Paul never seemed to get down. What was his secret? Prayer support! The same kind of prayer support that you can and must give to spiritual leaders you know.

So what happened as those early Christians prayed for Paul? Not surprisingly God heard their prayers and answered them in wonderful ways. Paul was *refreshed.* Luke reports that Paul was received warmly in Jerusalem and that they praised God for the report of his ministry to the Gentiles (Acts 21:17). He was *protected.* In Jerusalem he was falsely accused, dragged out of the temple by an angry crowd, arrested by Roman troops, and was nearly torn to pieces by the Sanhedrin. But with a plot to kill him hanging over his head, he was whisked away under the protection of 200 soldiers and cavalry, twice protected by Roman courts of law against the lies of Jewish leaders, spared death when a hurricane wrecked the ship he was on, and supernaturally protected against a poisonous snake bite on the island of Malta. Paul must have had quite a cadre of guardian angels. And his ministry was certainly *fruitful*. He was able to deliver the gifts designated for Jerusalem's poor (Acts 24:17)—something for which he had asked prayer. As for the rest of his "fruit," the New Testament record is itself the best evidence of the fruitfulness of his ministry and the answers to so many prayers.

Does interceding for spiritual leaders really make all that much difference? Absolutely! Peter Wagner once reminded a group of prayer leaders that "intercession for spiritual leaders is the most underutilized source of power in the church today." If he is right, then we have work to do—intercessory work; it's work that will make a huge difference for leaders and those they serve. Let's make sure that that power gets utilized!

Something to **Think** About

- On a scale of 1–7 (with 7 as the strongest value), how important do you think intercession for spiritual leaders was in Paul's mind? Explain your choice. How important is it to you?

- Are the ways that we need to intercede for spiritual leaders today different than those in Paul's day? If so how?

- From what do spiritual leaders today need to be *protected*? What is hindering *fruitful ministry*? What is robbing today's leaders of *joy and refreshment*?

- What positive results do you see in the lives of spiritual leaders today as a result of intercessory prayer?

Something to **Pray** About

- *Praise* our supreme spiritual leader, Jesus Christ, and all that He is doing through human leaders today.
- *Thank* God for the power, grace, and protection He provides for spiritual leaders through the prayers of His people.
- *Ask* the Spirit to reveal to you the pain and strain of the spiritual leaders you know so that you can step into it with them through your intercessory prayers.
- If you have sinned "against the Lord by failing to pray" for spiritual leaders (1 Samuel 12:23), *confess* that to the Lord and *commit* yourself to increased intercession for them.

Something to **Act** On

Invite the Holy Spirit to identify the spiritual leaders for whom He would have you pray. Regularly ask God to provide them spiritual protection, fruitful ministries, and spiritual refreshment. Add to your prayers for them the kinds of graces mentioned in Paul's recorded prayers (see chapter 15 in this book).

CHAPTER 18

The World Lives by Uplifted Hands

Seek the peace and prosperity of the city to which I have carried you into exile. Pray to the LORD for it, because if it prospers, you too will prosper. —Jeremiah 29:7

I urge, then, first of all, that requests, prayers, intercession and thanksgiving be made for everyone—for kings and all those in authority, that we may live peaceful and quiet lives in all godliness and holiness. —1 Timothy 2:1–2

I will proclaim the decree of the LORD: He said to me, "You are my Son; today I have become your Father. Ask of me, and I will make the nations your inheritance, the ends of the earth your possession. —Psalm 2:7–8

God has placed the destiny of the world in the hands of believers. Yes, this is God's world, but He has given us a responsibility for what happens in it. He has authorized us to rule the world along with His Son. The most critical element of our ongoing "rule" is sustained, fervent intercessory prayer. God can bless the world through our intercessory prayer.

When Christ teaches us to pray that God's "will be done on earth as it is in heaven" (Matthew 6:10), He has in mind the whole world and everything that happens in it. God wants the world to function as He intended, and prayer is a means to that end. Paul urged that "requests, prayers, intercession and thanksgiving be made for everyone" (1 Timothy 2:2). God urged Jewish exiles to pray for Babylon because, He said, "if it prospers, you too will prosper" (Jeremiah 29:7). Moses' prayers kept God's wrath from destroying the nation of Israel (Exodus 32:9–14; Psalm 106:23). Our intercessory prayers can accomplish these kinds of things today and much more. They can release grace, foster peace, restrain evil, protect innocents, avert disasters, enforce justice, and increase harvests. Helmut Thielecki writes, "The globe itself lives and is upheld as by Atlas arms through the prayers of those whose love has not grown cold. The world lives by these uplifted hands, and by nothing else!"[1]

The impact of our intercessory prayers can cover our neighbors, our cities, our leaders, our nations, and the whole of creation. Let's start by thinking about interceding for our *neighbors*. Jesus taught us to love our neighbors. Intercessory prayer is a powerful way to express our love for neighbors. It's a gift of time and energy that releases God's power and grace into their lives. Our neighbors include those who live near us, those who work near us, as well as those we meet in the rounds of our daily activities. There are countries were workers greet each other by saying, "God bless your work!" That probably won't work in most of our Western countries. But what if in meeting our neighbors we would breathe a silent prayer: "God bless their work!" or "God bless their home!" or "God bless this business!" That would be a prayer for them if it were truly directed to God. God wants the world of your neighbors to function as He intended. He wants us to pray for that.

Another world to pray for is the world of our *towns and cities*. As Jesus looked over the city of Jerusalem on the day of His triumphal entry, we are told that "he wept over it" (Luke 19:41). Luke's chosen word for "weep" means a loud agonizing cry of the soul. Jesus was moved with such a deep and compassionate concern for Jerusalem that it gave rise to an agonizing cry! At another time Jesus was moved with compassion by crowds of people as He visited towns and villages, because they were "harassed and helpless, like sheep without a shepherd" (Matthew 9:36). Jesus still weeps over towns, villages, and cities today. He sees hurting, helpless, unloved people who don't know where to turn for the help they need. As sensitive Christians we weep with Him and carry something of His burden for the cities where we live—burdens that press us to our knees.

Rulers and authorities also need our prayer support. Paul reminds us that government leaders are established by God (Romans 13:1). He instructs Timothy to teach his people to pray for "for kings and all those in authority" (1 Timothy 2:2). Most leaders bear heavy burdens. They exert powerful influence. Their decisions affect many lives. They need prayer support. God holds us responsible to intercede for them—for wisdom, health, protection, strength, endurance, patience, and much more. "Authorities" includes leaders in all places of prominence, such as business, education, government, health, media, and the military, as well as the church. Of course we will pray for the conversion of leaders, but our prayers will go far beyond that. God wants non-Christian leaders to live honorable lives and to accomplish His purposes. For that they need His grace—grace released through our intercessory prayers. And, says Paul, the result of our prayers for leaders will be "that we may live peaceful and quiet lives in all godliness and holiness."

God also expects us to pray for *nations*. As I write, there are 237 nations in the world. In Psalm 2:8, God the Father speaks to His Messiah Son and says: "Today I have become your Father. Ask of me, and I will make the nations your inheritance, the ends of the earth your possession." Today, exalted at the right hand of the Father (Hebrews 8:1–2), Jesus is gaining possession of the nations not by means of force but by intercession—His own constant intercession and the faithful intercessory prayers of believers. Together with Christ we pray for harvest workers, for the growth of His church, for the spread of the gospel, for the building of the kingdom, and the accomplishment of His will on earth. Together with Christ we pray for the demise of satanic strongholds rooted in unjust laws, false religions, perverted cultural practices, and doctrines of demons. We are "made . . . to be a kingdom and priests" (Revelation 1:6) so that we can serve with Him in building His kingdom.

God wants us to bless the *whole world* through our prayers. Paul is clearly thinking worldwide when he urges that prayers be made "for everyone." In *The Message*, Eugene Peterson translates 1 Timothy 2:1–2: "The first thing I want you to do is pray. Pray every way you know how, for everyone you know." No generation has ever had as much knowledge about world conditions and problems as ours. Along with that knowledge there comes a responsibility to pray far and wide for the establishment of God's plan and purposes.

We are very limited in what we can do for our world, but with intercession we have the option of making a humongous difference. Eugene Peterson writes these incisive words regarding the value of our intercession: "Far more of our nation's life is shaped by prayer than is formed by legislation. That we have not collapsed into anarchy is due more to prayer than to the police. . . . That society continues to be livable and that hope continues to be resurgent are attributable to prayer far more than to business prosperity or a flourishing of the arts. The single most important action contributing to whatever health and strength there is in our land is prayer."[2]

We are instruments in God's hands: royal priests whom He asks to partner with His Son to rule His world and establish His kingdom. What a high calling!

Something to **Think** About

- Which of the worlds mentioned in this chapter do you already pray for? Which ones do you seldom pray for?

- Do most Christians believe that "the world lives by these uplifted hands, and by nothing else!"? What difference does such a belief make?

- Could it be that we are sinning if we fail to pray for the world (see 1 Samuel 12:23)?

Something to **Pray** About

- *Praise* God as the supreme and sovereign ruler of the universe.
- *Thank* God that we are privileged to be royal priests engaged in intercessory work in the service of Jesus Christ, our great High Priest.
- If you have failed to intercede for your world, *confess* that and seek God's forgiveness.
- *Ask* God for the passion and strength to be an effective intercessor for your world.
- *Commit* yourself to being an intercessor for the world.

Something to Act On

Make intercessory prayer for neighbors, cities, authorities, nations, and the world a regular part of your prayer life. Be as specific and systematic as possible. Pray with the absolute assurance that something will happen because you prayed that wouldn't have happened if you hadn't prayed.

CHAPTER 19

The Power of Praying Together

Again, I tell you that if two of you on earth agree about anything you ask for, it will be done for you by my Father in heaven. For where two or three come together in my name, there am I with them.
—Matthew 18:19–20

They all joined together constantly in prayer. —Acts 1:14

They raised their voices together in prayer to God. —Acts 4:24

Intercessory praying can be done alone or collectively. Both forms of prayer are meant to be part of the believer's life. Jesus sometimes prayed alone, and at other times He prayed with His disciples. Believers in the early church also engaged in both forms of prayer. The book of Acts records thirteen occasions of personal prayer and twenty-four occasions of collective prayer. Unfortunately, most of the praying in the Western church today is personal prayer and very little of it is corporate prayer.

Praying together was a way of life for the first believers. A few hours after Jesus ascended to heaven, those early believers were in an upper room all joining together devotedly in prayer (Acts 1:14). Not long after that they were together devoting themselves "to the apostles' teaching and to the fellowship, to the breaking of bread *and to prayer*" (Acts 2:42, emphasis added). When the church's leaders were threatened, Luke reports that "they raised their voices together in prayer to God" (Acts 4:24). Clearly, the foundations of the early church were laid in united intercessory prayer.

Jesus laid the groundwork for united prayer when He said, "I tell you that if two of you on earth agree about anything you ask for, it will be done for you by my Father in heaven. For where two or three come together in my name, there am I with them" (Matthew 18:19–20). These verses suggest that Jesus expected at least four things to be true in the church He founded.

He expected that believers would *come together for prayer.* His followers were not just a gathering of isolated believers who enjoyed each other's company. They were a community of persons who belonged to each other, who needed each other, and who needed to express their "agreeing" prayers together before the throne of God. United prayer was to be fundamental to the life and well-being of the church. Jesus knowingly built united prayer into the DNA of the church.

Second, Jesus expected that believers would gather "*in his name.*" Their prayer meetings will be in His honor and for His purposes. They will enjoy His presence, be strengthened by His power, and claim His promises. As they gather in Jesus' name they will also pray "in his name." Their united prayers will be a visible confirmation of their spiritual union with him.

Jesus further expected that believers would *ask for themselves.* The form of the verb "ask" in the original language has the meaning, "ask *for ourselves.*" Jesus is not promising that the Father will give them solutions to social problems or meet community needs if they can agree on what to ask. Jesus' promise has to do with the kinds of things they need individually or corporately from God for their own spiritual well-being—things "according to his will," things "for life and godliness" (1 John 5:14–15; 2 Peter 1:3).

Finally, Jesus expected that believers would *agree on what to ask for*. The prayer meetings He envisioned were not simply people praying their personal prayers in a group setting. He envisioned people praying "agreeing" prayers with a Spirit-given unity of heart and mind. The word that Jesus used for "agree" means "to sound together, to harmonize." It's the word from which we get our English word "symphony." As agreeing prayers register in the ears of the Father they sound together, or harmonize. Jesus valued agreement in prayer. He is saying, "I am pleased when, coming together in My name, you discern My will and claim what I have promised by agreeing in prayer. The Father will surely respond to that kind of praying."

How do we come to know and agree on what to ask for? The answer is: by the Word and the Spirit. Jesus said, "If you remain in me and *my words* remain in you, ask whatever you wish, and it will be given you" (John 15:7, emphasis added). Jesus also promised that the Spirit would guide us into all truth (John 16:13). Guided by the Spirit and with Jesus' words in us, we will know and agree on what to ask for. We will ask for things such as "the grace of the Lord Jesus Christ, and the love of God, and the fellowship of the Holy Spirit" (2 Corinthians 13:14). We will plead for wisdom, knowledge, insight, and understanding. We will be led to ask for strength, holiness, and fruitfulness. We will ask to be clothed with "compassion, kindness, humility, gentleness and patience" (Colossians 3:12). We will desire and ask for the Spirit's fruit of "love, joy, peace, patience, kindness, goodness, faithfulness, gentleness and self-control (Galatians 5:22–23). We will ask for all these things and more, with each other and for each other, as our prayers "sound together" before the Father.

Jesus makes two promises to those who pray in this way. First, He promises *to be with us*. The greatest wonder of agreeing prayer is not in the numbers who come together, nor in the prayers prayed, or even the agreement in those prayers. The greatest wonder is in the Person who comes to be present with us. The presence of Jesus assures the unity, and the agreement, and ultimately the promised answer. What an amazing thing when you think of it. The most holy, most mighty, King of kings, and Lord of the universe comes to join any group of believers who meet in His name no matter how small, or weak, or insignificant. Wow! What an incredible honor!

Second, Jesus promises that His *Father in heaven will do what is asked*. This seems to say that God will do anything we want Him to if only we can get someone to agree with us and ask for it with us. That is not what is promised. What the Father will do for us is anything we ask that is in accord with His will, anything that we know to be in Jesus' name and confidently ask for together with other believers. What an amazing promise.

These words of Jesus are especially encouraging to believers who pray together in various ways. Believing *husbands and wives* who pray together can confidently ask for the grace to love and respect each other (Ephesians 5:33). *Families* that pray together will claim spiritual riches for their circle of nearness and will foster deepening levels of love and concern. The members of *prayer support groups* will be able to give each other bracing prayer support and help each other grow spiritually. *Ministry groups* who claim the promise of agreeing prayer will receive God's wisdom and strength for their ministry activities. Finally, *worshipers* who come together in Jesus' name can ask and receive the help they need to worship God in spirit and in truth (John 4:24).

Andrew Murray, reflecting on these words of Jesus in Matthew

18, says: "What an unspeakable privilege united prayer is, and what a power it might be. If the believing husband and wife knew that they were joined together in the name of Jesus to experience His presence and power in united prayer; if friends believed what mighty help two or three praying in concert could give each other; if in every church united effectual prayer were regarded as one of the chief purposes for which they are banded together, the highest exercise of their power as a church—who can say what blessing might come to and through those who thus agreed to prove God in the fulfillment of His promise."[1] That "unspeakable privilege" is one of the Father's absolutely wonderful gifts to us, His children. Don't miss it!

Something to **Think** About

- Why do you think Jesus made this promise? On a scale of 1–10 (10 being highest) how important did Jesus think it was for believers to pray together?

- What role does the Bible have in helping us come to agreement in prayer? What role does the Holy Spirit have? What role does Jesus have?

- Do most people you know in the Christian community agree with Andrew Murray that united prayer is "an unspeakable privilege?" Do you?

- How can a church today live out the expectations of Christ that believers would meet together and pray agreeing prayers?

Something to **Pray** About

- *Praise* Jesus as the omnipresent One who is present whenever and wherever believers come together in His name.
- *Thank* the Father for graciously and willingly providing all that we need for life and godliness in response to our asking.
- *Confess*, for yourself and for your spiritual community, any failure in united prayer that you are aware of.
- *Ask* God to give you and other believers "agreeing prayer" experiences.
- *Commit* to united prayer with other believers.

Something to **Act** On

If you are involved in united prayer with other Christians, make sure that you are practicing agreeing prayer with each other and claiming spiritual riches for each other at least some of the time that you are together.

CHAPTER 20

The Devil Trembles When We Pray

Lead us not into temptation, but deliver us from the evil one.

—Matthew 6:13

His disciples asked him [Jesus] privately, "Why couldn't we drive it [a demon] out?" He replied, "This kind can come out only by prayer."

—Mark 9:28–29

Simon, Simon, Satan has asked to sift you as wheat. But I have prayed for you, Simon, that your faith may not fail. And when you have turned back, strengthen your brothers." —Luke 22:31–32

One of my favorite quotes on spiritual warfare comes from *The Kneeling Christian*: "There is nothing the devil dreads so much as prayer? His great concern is to keep us from praying. Someone has wisely said, 'Satan laughs at our toiling, mocks at our wisdom, but trembles when we pray.'"[1] The phrase I like best says, Satan "trembles when we pray." Even though I like the phrase, I find it hard to imagine that Satan trembles when I pray. Can *my* prayers really make him tremble? But then, when I remember what God does when I pray, I understand. You see, it's not us or our prayers that Satan fears. It's Christ that he fears. He dreads prayer because he dreads what Christ does when we pray. He knows that Christ hears and answers prayer. And that spells trouble for him.

Prayer is our supreme weapon against evil. By prayer we can thwart Satan's attacks, foil his schemes, and lessen his effectiveness. By prayer we assault the devil's strongholds, build the kingdom of God, send workers into the harvest fields, and open doors for the gospel. Prayer, real prayer, is Satan's undoing. He does not know how to cope with prayer. That's why he works so hard to keep us from praying.

Wesley Duewel defines warfare prayer as "joining Christ in driving out and defeating Satan and in setting his captives free. It is advancing against Satan's strongholds and dislodging and expelling demon forces."[2] Two elements in this definition are particularly important. First, Duewel emphasizes that warfare prayer is "joining Christ" in His victory over the forces of hell. Christ is the one conquering Satan, not us. We are cooperating with Him, not He with us. He won the victory on the cross. We are pitching in with the mop-up operation. Second, Duewel underscores the crucial fact that the battle is primarily offensive: moving out against Satan and reclaiming what is rightfully Christ's.

The conflict between good and evil, between God and the devil, is a consistent theme throughout the Bible. Christ's coming to earth moved the battle to a whole new level. John stresses that "the reason the Son of God appeared was to destroy the devil's work" (1 John 3:8). Luke summarizes Jesus' life and ministry by saying, "He went around doing good and healing all who were under the power of the devil" (Acts 10:38). Paul disclosed the "how" of Christ's victory: "Having disarmed the powers and authorities, he made a public spectacle of them, triumphing over them by the cross" (Colossians 2:15). Jesus, on his way to the cross, foresaw that His death would have both a repelling and an attracting effect. He said: "Now the prince of this world will be driven out. But I, when I am lifted up from the earth, will draw all men to myself" (John 12:31–32). Christ, who won these victories on earth, now continues to enforce His victory from heaven through the intercessory prayers of believers. And, as the finale approaches, the God of peace is going to "soon crush Satan under your feet" (Romans 16:20).

There are several Bible passages that clearly link intercessory prayer and spiritual warfare. The one we are probably most familiar with comes at the end of the Lord's Prayer where Jesus teaches us to pray, "Deliver us from the evil one." Jesus understood the reality and the power of evil in the world. He knew that we would need constant protection, so He urges us to make prayer for deliverance a regular part of our prayer lives. Near the end of His life Jesus practiced this very thing when He asked the Father not to take His disciples out of the world but to "protect them from the evil one" (John 17:15). Spiritual deliverance depends on constant prevailing prayer.

On another occasion, after Jesus disciples had failed to cast out a demon, they asked Him, "Why couldn't we drive it out"? Jesus answered, "This kind can come out only by prayer" (Mark 9:28–29). Jesus was reminding them, and us, that we do not have the ability to defeat forces of evil in our own power. That power belongs to God, and God's hand is moved through our prayers. Christ wants us to pray so that He can gain the victory. Satan would like to have us try to win the victory in our own strength—for obvious reasons.

A short time before Simon Peter's denial, Jesus said to him, "Simon, Simon, Satan has asked to sift you as wheat. But I have prayed for you, Simon, that your faith may not fail. And when you have turned back, strengthen your brothers" (Luke 22:31–32). What's surprising in this account is that Jesus does not ask the Father to deny Satan's request to sift Peter. He allows the test, which was somehow for Peter's benefit. Peter had to come to grips with what was in his heart—with the arrogance that made him think that he was stronger than all the other disciples and with the fear that gave rise to his denial. But Jesus prayed and, as a result, Peter's faith did not fail. Satan's sifting brought him insight and healing. Peter gained a victory and was able afterward to strengthen his brothers. Satan's plan was derailed by Jesus' prayer.

Intercession was also the key to winning battles over the powers of evil in the early years of the church. When commanded not to speak in Jesus' name and threatened with harm if they did, the believers of Jerusalem "raised their voices together in prayer to God." They asked to be able to "speak [the] word with great boldness" and to "heal and perform miraculous signs and wonders" (Acts 4:29–30). What happened? Just what you would expect! God heard and answered. They spoke the word with boldness. They "performed many miraculous signs and wonders among the people" and "more and more men and women believed in the Lord. . . . Crowds gathered . . . bringing their sick and those tormented by evil spirits, and all of them were healed" (Acts 5:12–16). What a victory that was! Satan was defeated, his territory invaded, and his captives were released. That's spiritual warfare by means of intercession.

Our struggle, said Paul, is "against the rulers, against the authorities, against the power of this dark world and against the spiritual forces of evil in the heavenly realms." Paul ends his somber depiction of the operations of evil in the world by calling us to "be alert and always keep on praying for all the saints" (Ephesians 6:12, 18). The weapon of prayer is a strong weapon that God has placed in our hands in order to come against the invisible forces of evil that operate in our world today. Our prayers move the arm of God, move His arms to destroy works of the devil. Satan can deal with most everything we come at him with, but he cannot deal with the arm of the Lord moved through prayer. You can be sure that the "saints" you know are under attack, and they need your sustaining prayers.

Let me end by encouraging you to join Christ in driving out and defeating Satan. Ask Him for the resolve to faithfully pray, "Deliver us from the evil one." Ask for the Spirit's help to "always keep on praying for all the saints," starting with those who are nearest and dearest to you. Ask God to give you a holy boldness and strong faith as you join Him in setting captives free. You have nothing to loose, and everything to gain.

Something to **Think** About

- Can you imagine Satan trembling when you pray? Why or why not?

- What would you say to a person who says, "I am not going to engage in warfare prayer, because I don't want the devil to target me?" *The devil has already got a hold of him by not praying.*

- What is Satan doing right now to keep believers from warfare prayer? What could you do to change that?

  Good Question - My Question

- It's possible to give too much attention to the devil or too little attention. It's wise to give him about as much attention as he gets in the Bible. How does the amount of attention you give him compare to that of the Bible?

Something to **Pray** About

- *Praise* Christ as the mighty conqueror of sin and Satan.
- *Thank* God for sending His Son, Jesus Christ, to deliver us from the evil one.
- If you have failed to engage the enemy in warfare prayer, *confess* that to the Lord and ask His forgiveness.
- *Ask* for the Spirit to help you be alert to the devil's schemes and to keep on praying for all the saints.
- *Commit* yourself to praying for the devil's defeat and the release of his captives.

Something to **Act** On

Give some serious thought to what Satan is trying to do in your life. In your relationships. In the lives of your family members. In your faith community. Pray warfare prayers with an awareness of what Christ wants to do to counteract Satan.

CHAPTER 21

The Prayer of Faith Moves Mountains

Your disciples . . . could not heal him [boy with demon]. The disciples
came to Jesus in private and asked, "Why couldn't we drive it [the de-
mon] out?" He replied, "Because you have so little faith. I tell you the
truth, if you have faith as small as a mustard seed, you can say to this
mountain, 'Move from here to there' and it will move. Nothing will be
*impossible for you." —*Matthew 17:16, 19–21

If any of you lacks wisdom, he should ask God, who gives generously to
all without finding fault, and it will be given him. But when he asks, he
must believe and not doubt, because he who doubts is like a wave of the
sea, blown and tossed by the wind. That man should not think he will
*receive anything from the Lord. —*James 1:5–7

The prayer that moves mountains is a prayer of faith. Faith is the
key factor in our salvation. It is also a key factor in prayer. Jesus
regularly connected prayer with faith, and He wanted His disciples,
and all believers, to understand the importance of praying in faith.

Since there are many false ideas of what faith is, let me begin
by saying what faith is not. Faith is not an inner conviction that
something will happen if only I strongly believe that it will. It is
not confidence that prayer works. It is not clinging tenaciously to

an impossible dream until it is realized. It is not a way to try to get God to act when, and where, and how I please. It is not the ability to move a mountain of my choice because I want it moved. The problem with all of these concepts of faith is that they are centered in something other than God.

Faith is confidence in God. A prayer of faith is a prayer of absolute confidence that God will do, in response to our asking, what He wants to do in order to advance His kingdom. We know from the Bible, for example, that God wants to give wisdom to Christians. So if we ask for wisdom with absolute confidence, we will receive it. If we do not ask or if we ask without such confidence, we will not receive it (James 1:5–7).

We don't know from the Bible whether or not God wants to move this or that mountain, or to do something that is as difficult as moving a mountain. If, however, He reveals to us by His Spirit that He wants to move a mountain, then we can ask for that to happen with absolute confidence and it will. Jesus said, "If you have faith as small as a mustard seed, you can say to this mountain, 'Move from here to there' and it will move" (Matthew 17:20–21). The small faith that asks has absolute confidence that God wants to and is able to move that mountain. So it asks and God complies. I can only pray such a prayer of faith if I know what it is that God wants to do. The burden of proof is on knowing God's will. It's impossible for me to ask in faith if I don't believe it is God's will to do what I am asking.

In the prayer of faith, the focus must be on God. It is being sure that God always acts in character, and in accord with His will and His promises. Strong faith comes from being occupied with God, conscious of His will, His ways, His love, and His grace. A person of faith knows that God is alive, that He hears, that He is all powerful, that He acts in history, and that He wants to respond to prayer.

A person of faith is fully persuaded that God can and will do what He has promised. Of Abraham—a hero of faith—scripture says, he "was strengthened in his faith and gave glory to God, being fully persuaded that God had power to do what he had promised" (Romans 4:20–21).

Let's try for a moment to think of the prayer of faith from God's perspective. God wants to act powerfully, wisely, and lovingly in the world to build His kingdom and accomplish His will. Since He has chosen to link His activities in the world to the prayers of His people, He is alert to persons of faith who, knowing Him and His heart, will ask Him to do the very things He wants to do in order to build His kingdom. Finding such persons He reveals His intention to them in advance so they can ask what He has shown them. Then He listens to their prayers of faith and acts in response to them. When they ask, even if it is for something as difficult as moving a mountain, He acts in response to those prayers.

What will God do in response to our prayers of faith? He will do that which brings glory to His name, advances His kingdom, and is in accord with His will (Matthew 6:9–10). He will do anything along these lines within the limits of His capability. And since He is almighty there is no limit to what He can do. He can make the sun stall in its orbit, make rivers dry up, still a storm, or move a mountain. When these things happen the issue is not the size of the faith of the person asking. A mustard-seed-size faith will do. The issue is the unlimited power of God.

The confidence that faith has in God is necessary when we are praying for ourselves too. To blind Bartimaeus, who pleaded with Jesus for His sight, Jesus said, "Go . . . your faith has healed you" (Mark 10:52). To the sick woman who touched His garments and found herself healed, Jesus said, "Daughter, your faith has healed you. Go in peace and be freed from your suffering" (Mark 5:34). And to a sinful woman who had anointed Jesus' feet while He was eating at a Pharisee's home, Jesus first said, "Your sins are forgiven," and then a few moments later said, "Your faith has saved you; go in peace" (Luke 7:48, 50). Each of these had faith to receive from Jesus the healing that He was eager to give.

Faith is also necessary when we are praying for others. Jesus sometimes healed people in response to the faith of those who prayed for them. The most surprising case is that of the men who got their paralytic friend to Jesus through a hole in the roof of the house where He was teaching. Mark tells us, "When Jesus saw *their* faith"—the faith of the friends lowering the mat that the man was lying on—He forgave the man's sin and healed him (Mark 2:5–12, emphasis added). A Roman centurion (Matthew 8:5–13), a synagogue leader (Mark 5:22–43), and a Canaanite woman (Matthew 15:28) were all granted their requests for others because of their faith. God delights to bestow blessings on others in response to our prayers of faith.

Lack of faith can cause prayer to fail. Jesus was often disappointed at lack of faith. Five times He exclaimed, "O you of little faith." Three times He rebuked listeners as an "unbelieving generation." He was amazed at the lack of faith of the people in His hometown and, as a result, could do no miracles (Mark 6:6). Even the disciples failed at one point to pray in faith. In the absence of Jesus, they were unable to help a boy oppressed by a demon because they didn't have faith (Matthew 17:20; Mark 9:29). God is almighty and unlimited in what He chooses to do. But to the extent that He has chosen to work in response to faith prayers, He declines to work when there is lack of faith.

How can we grow in the faith that we need to pray effectively? The first thing we can do is to *ask* God for it. Since God wants us to have faith, we can ask for faith with the assurance that He will grant it. That's a prayer in accord with His will (1 John 5:14–15). We can and should also immerse ourselves in the Word of God. Paul said, "Faith comes from hearing the message, and the message is heard through the word of Christ" (Romans 10:17). In God's Word we have everything necessary to inform and increase our faith. From the Word we learn what it is that God wants to do for us and what He wants to do to build His kingdom. Knowing that is foundational to faith.

Something to **Think** About

- When you intercede do you tend to think of God as reluctant to give or eager to give? What difference would how you think of God make when you pray?

- How should we go about deciding what to pray for? Are there things we shouldn't pray for?

- What things in your life tend to strengthen the faith that you bring to prayer? What things tend to weaken faith?

Something to **Pray** About

- *Praise* God for the wisdom with which He hears and answers prayer.
- *Thank* God for His answers to your prayers. Be as specific as possible.
- If you have asked without faith, *confess* that to the Lord and acknowledge that you have limited His working.

- *Ask* God to give you the faith to ask in accord with His will with absolute confidence.
- *Commit* to spiritual disciplines that will grow your faith life.

Something to **Act** On

Ask God to show you what it is that He wants to do in your family, in your church, in your community, or even in His worldwide kingdom. Pray with absolute confidence for anything that He confirms in your heart as His will.

CHAPTER 22

The Power of Persistent Prayer

Then he [Jesus] said to them, "Suppose one of you has a friend, and he goes to him at midnight and says, 'Friend, lend me three loaves of bread, because a friend of mine on a journey has come to me, and I have nothing to set before him.'

Then the one inside answers, 'Don't bother me. The door is already locked, and my children are with me in bed. I can't get up and give you anything.' I tell you, though he will not get up and give him the bread because he is his friend, yet because of the man's boldness he will get up and give him as much as he needs. —Luke 11:5–8

Epaphras, who is one of you and a servant of Christ Jesus . . . is always wrestling in prayer for you, that you may stand firm in all the will of God, mature and fully assured. —Colossians 4:12

The New Testament places a great emphasis on persistent prayer. Jesus thought it was so important that He pressed the lesson of persistence home in two separate parables: the parable of the persistent widow (Luke 18:1–8) and the parable of the friend at midnight (Luke 11:5–8). In the friend-at-midnight story, Jesus encourages His followers to approach heaven's door like a shameless neighbor who, despite an initial refusal, continues to knock on his neighbor's door until he gets the bread he needs for his friend. "Because of the man's boldness," says Jesus, "he will get up and give him as much as he needs."

In His friend-at-midnight story, Jesus was not just urging prayer. He was urging bold, persistent prayer. Jesus wants us to understand that there is a difference between casual prayer and bold prayer. Casual prayer is weak and ineffective, lacking earnestness and perseverance. Bold prayer is shamelessly urgent and unrelenting in its concern to obtain God's provision for a needy person. It is unwilling to take no for an answer. It stands ready to push through all obstacles. That's the kind of intercessory prayer that God is pleased with.

God is not pleased, however, with the kind of persistent prayer that attempts to coerce Him into doing what we want. We can't make God do anything, and, even if we could, we wouldn't want to. The world would be a sorry place if our wills could prevail over God's will. The truth is, however, that God is very willing to act in line with our prayers if our prayers are in line with His will. Richard C. Trench said, "We must not conceive of prayer as an overcoming of God's reluctance, but a laying hold of his highest willingness."[1] You can even turn that around and say that bold intercession is God's way of laying hold of our reluctance in order to move us to claim His willingness. We don't prevail over God; He prevails over us.

The apostle Paul also understood the value of persistent prayer. He commends his coworker Epaphras to his Colossian readers as one who "is always wrestling in prayer for you that you may stand firm in all the will of God, mature and fully assured." The word Paul uses for "wrestling" has the meaning of striving, fighting, laboring earnestly, or persevering in the face of opposition. It was used in Paul's day to describe combatants who strained every nerve to win a victory. Our English word "agony" comes from the same root. The Colossians must have been awe-struck to think that they were being prayed for with such strain and pain. I imagine that they took stock of life at their church and discovered some evidences of Epaphras's wrestling prayers.

There are at least three important reasons for persistent prayer. The most important reason is *to see God's will accomplished on earth.* Through persistent prayer we partner with God in working out His eternal plan. Christ is responsible for implementing God's redemptive plan and defeating Satan, but He chooses to do so in response to our prayers. John Calvin taught that prayer was a means by which the power of Satan could be broken and God's kingdom extended.

A second important reason for persistent prayer is that *it moves the pray-er toward God.* Persistent prayer is waiting on God. When we wait on God, we get to be *with* God and we come to know Him better and better. We come to know that He is not like the cranky judge in Jesus' persistent-widow story (Luke 18:2) nor like the sleepy, reluctant neighbor in Jesus' friend-at-midnight story (Luke 11:7). We come to know that He is a gracious heavenly Father who is pleased to give good things to those who ask (Matthew 7:11). We come to know that He is "for us" and will "graciously give us all things" (Romans 8:31–32). We become so absorbed in *His* world that His will becomes our will; His priorities become our priorities; His focus becomes our focus. Persistent prayer changes us.

A third important reason for persistent prayer is *to bring us face to face with our own weaknesses and frailties.* As we wait on God to do what we cannot do, we realize anew that we are helpless creatures, doomed to fail without His help. We humbly admit that our best human efforts are inadequate. Andrew Murray said: "God holds back and seeks to get away from us until what is of flesh and self and laziness in us is overcome. Then we can prevail with Him so that He *can* and *must* bless us."[2] Coming to grips with our own impotence, we hold on to His omnipotence. Our faith muscles grow stronger, our spiritual stamina increases, and our prayers get refined. Through persistent prayer God humbles us, teaches us, trains us, and matures us.

Persistent prayer is very important, but it is not easy. Wesley Duewel reminds us: "Prevailing, wrestling prayer . . . can be the most difficult work you can do. It demands total sincerity, intense desire, full concentration, and whole-souled determination."[3] When we determine to pray with persistence, the world, the flesh, and the devil come against us. The *world*—life organized apart from God—comes against us by preempting our time and attention with a host of counterproductive values. The *flesh*—what remains in us of our sinful nature— "argues" against the time and the sacrifice that prayer requires. And the *devil* opposes our efforts at prayer "tooth and nail." But God is greater than this nasty trinity of opponents. With His help we can overcome these deadly hindrances and become bold, persistent intercessors.

Two things in particular make it possible for us to intercede with holy boldness. First, the energizing work of the Holy Spirit in our hearts. All true prayer is the result of the Spirit's work within us. All attempts to persist without His help are doomed to failure, for "we do not know what we ought to pray for." But with the Spirit's help we can succeed because He "helps us in our weakness" (Romans 8:26). At the same time the Spirit also imparts to us the holy longings of the Father, which in turn become the content of our prayers. Persistent prayer is a way of partnering with the Holy Spirit—He prompting, guiding, and energizing us; we listening, yielding, and wrestling in prayer.

Second, we are united with Jesus Christ, the ultimate persistent intercessor. Christ has been interceding for God's kingdom and

God's purposes from the beginning of time, uniquely so since the days of His incarnation and ascension to the Father's right hand. It is His ongoing ministry, His highest priority. You and I are invited to partner with Christ in His great ministry of intercession. What a privilege! What a glory! You may not feel up to it. But the Spirit who dwells in you is. He can turn you into the mighty, prevailing intercessor that God wants you to be. Praise the Lord!

Something to **Think** About

- How would you explain the difference between casual prayer and persistent prayer?

- Have you found the world, the flesh, or the devil opposing prayer in your life? How can this trinity of enemies be overcome?

- Has anyone been an Epaphras for you (see Colossians 4:12)? Is there someone for whom God might want you to be an Epaphras?

- Try to identify a God-concern in your world of experience that cries out for persistent prayer? What makes you sure it is a God-concern?

Something to **Pray** About

- *Praise* God for the wonderful way that He uses your prayers to accomplish His purposes.
- *Thank* God for the prayer partnership of Jesus Christ and the prayer help of the Holy Spirit.

- If the flesh or self or laziness has kept you from being a persistent intercessor, *confess* that to the Lord and find His forgiveness.
- *Ask* for the Holy Spirit's guidance and staying power as you persist in intercession.

Something to **Act** On

Invite the Holy Spirit to lead you to a God-concern on which to focus persistent prayer. What He gives you will undoubtedly be something that will glorify God's name and advance His kingdom. Once you have this God-concern, commit yourself to intercede boldly until the answer comes or until the Spirit prompts you to stop.

CHAPTER 23

Fasting Enhances Prayer

I, Daniel, . . . turned to the Lord God and pleaded with him in prayer and petition, in fasting, and in sackcloth and ashes. I prayed to the LORD *my God and confessed.* —Daniel 9:2–4

They said to me, . . . "The wall of Jerusalem is broken down, and its gates have been burned with fire." When I heard these things, I sat down and wept. For some days I mourned and fasted and prayed before the God of heaven. —Nehemiah 1:3–4

"Even now," declares the LORD, *"return to me with all your heart, with fasting and weeping and mourning." Rend your heart and not your garments.* —Joel 2:12–13

Biblical fasting is abstinence with a spiritual goal in mind. Though fasting can refer to voluntary abstinence from any necessity or pleasure of life for a period of time, in the Bible it usually refers to abstinence from food. The Hebrew word for fasting means to "cover the mouth." The Greek word means "not to eat."

The Bible does not command fasting, but it does bear witness to the fact that fasting was highly valued and regularly practiced by God's people in both the Old and New Testaments. When men and women of the Bible added fasting to their prayers, God honored their efforts in some pretty amazing ways. Moses, David, Ezra, Elijah, Daniel, Nehemiah, and Anna were all people who fasted. In their fasting and prayers, they gained great things from God. Jesus launched His earthly ministry with forty days of fasting and prayer in the wilderness. When Jesus spoke of fasting, He did not say, "if you fast," He said, "when you fast." He evidently expected fasting to be part of the normal believer's life.

Though fasting can be an aid to physical health, our concern in this chapter is with the spiritual benefits of biblical fasting. Scripture presents fasting as a spiritual exercise that is of great value for believers. Its value lies primarily in its ability to loosen our ties to the physical world and strengthen our ties to the heavenly world. Fasting is a way to say no to physical appetite and yes to spiritual appetite. Following are several ways in which fasting can contribute to the spiritual health and well-being of individual Christians or groups of believers.

Biblical fasting *enhances prayer.* Very often fasting and prayer are linked together in Bible references. Daniel pleaded with God "in prayer and petition, in fasting." The New Testament church commissioned Paul and Barnabas to the work to which they were called "after they had fasted and prayed" (Acts 13:3). Later Paul and Barnabas appointed and commissioned elders to the Lord "with prayer and fasting" (Acts 14:23). Fasting is a God-given strategy for deepening and strengthening our prayer lives. Fasting enhances earnest prayer by allowing us to detach from the physical and attach to the spiritual. It provides a means to gain increased control over the many hindrances that tend to diminish our prayer lives. If you want a better prayer life, fasting may be just the lift that you need.

Biblical fasting *helps us discern God's will.* The church leaders in Antioch understood this. While they were worshiping and fasting, the Holy Spirit said to them, "Set apart for me Barnabas and Saul for the work to which I have called them" (Acts 13:2). Nehemiah "mourned and fasted and prayed before the God of heaven" in order to get God's direction for rebuilding the walls of Jerusalem. Fasting will sharpen our spiritual hearing and make our hearts increasingly receptive to the Spirit's promptings. So if you have decisions to make and if your spiritual ears need opening, why not get God's guidance the way early Christians did—by prayer and fasting.

Biblical fasting *is a vehicle for self-examination*—a vehicle that often leads to repentance and confession. Fasting gives the Spirit opportunity to search our hearts and reveal our true spiritual condition. It's a useful tool for anyone who is deeply concerned to deal with a sin condition that may be hindering spiritual vitality. When Israel was confronted with a crisis brought on by their sin, God spoke through His prophet Joel and said, "'Return to me with all your heart, with fasting and weeping and mourning.' Rend your hearts and not your garments. Return to the LORD" (Joel 2:12–13). Israel's annual Day of Atonement also required fasting as an outward expression of inner repentance (Leviticus 16:29–31). Not once in all the records of scripture did God fail to come to the aid of those who fasted, prayed, and repented before Him.

Biblical fasting is *a God-ordained form of self-denial*. Jesus said to His disciples, "If anyone would come after me, he must deny himself and take up his cross and follow me" (Matthew 16:24). Self-denial often means self-sacrifice and suffering; not something that comes easily in our self-indulgent, pleasure-oriented world. But fasting can help. Fasting is a kind of doing without that helps train us to deal with appetites and drives that, if not properly controlled, will get us into sin trouble. Fasting works to counteract the self-indulgence so characteristic of the flesh and reinforces the kinds of self-disciplines instilled by the Spirit. We could use more of that today, don't you think?

Biblical fasting leads to *a closer walk with God*. It led to a deep spirituality for the prophetess Anna who, Luke tells us, "never left the temple but worshiped night and day, fasting and praying" (Luke 2:37). It led to intimacy with God for the disciples of John who often fasted and prayed for spiritual reasons (Luke 5:33). Fasting helps focus our attention on God and makes us more sensitive to Him and His workings in our lives. It takes our attention away from self and selfish pursuits. The ultimate value of a close walk with God comes when we can say with David, "you . . . fill me with joy in your presence, with eternal pleasures at your right hand" (Psalm 16:11).

Fasting can *fortify us in a crisis situation*. When Israel was threatened by a multinational army, King Jehoshaphat inquired of the Lord and "proclaimed a fast for all Judah." In response to His proclamation, fasting Israelites humbly acknowledged their dependence on God and said, "We do not know what to do, but our eyes are upon you" (2 Chronicles 20:3, 12). In response God gave them a great victory. When King Xerxes, giving in to Haman's hate-filled proposal, ordered that all the Jews of his empire were to be killed on a single day, Queen Esther, a Jew, called for a fast. "Go," she said to Mordecai, "gather together all the Jews who are in Susa, and fast for me. Do not eat or drink for three days, night or day. I and my maids will fast as you do" (Esther 4:16). Their fast, coupled with Esther's courage and King Xerxes' change of heart, resulted in deliverance for the Jews and triumph over their enemies. Crisis situations have a way of driving us to the Lord. Fasting keeps us centered on Him. Don't hesitate to add fasting to your urgent prayers when you face a troubling situation.

Finally, biblical fasting *provides a way to prepare for a mission*. Nehemiah prepared for his mission to rebuild the walls of Jerusalem by fasting and prayer (Nehemiah 1:4). Ezra prepared a contingent of Jews to migrate back to the Promised Land by means of a fast (Ezra 8:21). When the time came for Jesus to begin His earthly ministry, He fasted forty days and nights in the wilderness so that He might fully know the Father's will (Matthew 4:1–2). By means of fasting we not only come to know God's plan for our lives, but we are also moved to submit to His will.

Do you want to enhance your prayer life? Are you seeking God's guidance? Is there a sin in your life that needs to be rooted out? Could you use more spiritual discipline? Are you facing a troubling situation? Is God calling you to serve Him in some particular way? Fasting can help you make spiritual gains in any one or all of these areas. It's as valid today as it ever was. If you have tried to make spiritual gains in your own way and in your own strength but have failed, why not try God's way—fasting. He honors those who honor His ways. He did in the past. He will today!

Something to **Think** About

- Why do you think fasting is so closely linked with prayer? What is there about fasting that causes it to enhance prayer?

- Which of the seven benefits of fasting, explained in this chapter, might be most helpful to you right now? Explain.

- What do you think would happen if believers today took fasting as seriously as the believers of biblical days?

Something to **Pray** About

- *Thank* God for giving us the practice of fasting as a way to achieve spiritual strength and growth.
- *Ask* God to lead you into those fasting practices that would be of greatest benefit to you.
- If you have spurned fasting for wrong reasons, *confess* that to the Lord and find His forgiveness.
- *Commit* yourself to use any biblical fasting practice to which the Holy Spirit leads you.

Something to **Act** On

Decide when and where one of the above mentioned fasting practices will benefit you in your spiritual journey and then make use of it for that purpose. (Those who are new to fasting should begin gradually, with a single meal, a day, or a week before attempting a longer fast. Some persons with medical conditions should not fast unless it is done under a doctor's supervision.)

CHAPTER 24

Asking Leads to Action

You did not choose me, but I chose you and appointed you to go and bear fruit—fruit that will last. Then the Father will give you whatever you ask in my name. —John 15:16

"O Lord, let your ear be attentive to the prayer of this your servant. . . . Give your servant success today by granting him favor in the presence of this man."

The king said to me, "What is it you want?"

Then I prayed to the God of heaven, and I answered the king, "If it pleases the king . . . let him send me to the city in Judah where my fathers are buried so that I can rebuild it." —Nehemiah 1:11, 2:4–5

God wants more than asking. He also wants action. Intercessory prayer and action go hand in hand. Prayer needs to be linked to action; action needs to be linked to prayer. God's way of getting His work done in the world is prayer combined with action and action combined with prayer.

There is a sense in which *prayer is action*. It is action because our act of prayer causes God to move in the lives of the persons or the events we pray for. God acts when we pray, not because He has to, but because He chooses to. He has promised to act in response to prayer in order to accomplish His purpose on earth. Our intercessory prayers, then, are acts that advance the kingdom of God and restrain the forces of evil in the world. Jim Wallis wanted to teach the readers of *Sojourner* magazine to think of prayer as action. He said of intercession: "It is a prayer *for* salvation, healing, peace, righteousness, justice, protection and well-being. It is a prayer *against* sin, unrighteousness, idolatry, injustice and calamity."[1] This kind of prayer is a human action that moves the hand of God to supernatural action.

Intercessory prayer *prepares us for action.* Nehemiah, concerned for the broken-down walls of Jerusalem, mourned, fasted, and prayed. Then, when opportunity arose, he said to King Artaxerxes, "Send me to the city in Judah where my fathers are buried so that I can rebuild it" (Nehemiah 2:5). When the king granted his request, Nehemiah's prayer turned into action. Prayer primed the king to accede to his request. Prayer prepared Nehemiah for his leadership role in rebuilding the walls of Jerusalem. Intercessory prayer often works that way. It becomes the launching pad for action. It opens our minds to hear what it is that God wants us to do. It becomes God's way of preparing us and equipping us to be part of the answer.

Intercessory prayer *will lead us into action.* Prayer was never meant to be an excuse to do nothing. There is good advice in the comment recalled by C. Samuel Storms, "When you pray, don't give instructions—report for duty!"[2] God can, of course, answer our prayers in wonderful and supernatural ways completely without our involvement. But His normal way of working is through human instruments, weak as we are. He often chooses to make us part of the answer. Nehemiah seems to have found this combination of prayer and action. "We prayed to our God," he said, "and posted a guard day and night to meet this threat" (Nehemiah 4:9). As you pray for people who have needs, be prepared to meet needs that God brings to your attention.

As you pray for the lost, tell God you are ready and willing to share the good news with anyone He brings into your life if the opportunity arises. As you pray for material needs of kingdom ministries, reach for your checkbook. Don't expect the Lord to honor your prayers if you are not willing to be the answer to those prayers.

Intercessory prayer *sustains us in action.* At the very time that Jesus' disciples were sure they could not carry on without Him. He assured them that they could, because they could pray. "Anyone who has faith in me," He said, "will do what I have been doing" and "even greater things . . . because I am going to the Father. And I will do whatever you ask in my name" (John 14:12–13). He who would do the works of God must be linked by prayer to the Son of God. Prayer is the channel through which God's empowering grace flows to those who are busy in His service. Praying, working disciples will find Christ working in and through them to bring glory to the Father. The end result will be great works—works like those Jesus did when He was on earth.

Intercessory prayer *makes ready the way for action.* When we lay a foundation of prayer, God goes before us. In response to Nehemiah's prayer, God prepared King Artaxerxes, whom he served, to notice his sad look, to ask him for an explanation, and then to say yes to Nehemiah's preposterous proposal to rebuild the walls of Jerusalem. Prayer opened the door for action. In the prayer-care-share ministry promoted by the *Mission America Coalition,* believers are taught to pray for, care for, and share Christ with their neighbors. The team leading that ministry has noticed that, again and again, prayer starts the ministry-ball rolling. Prayer leads to a next step—caring—and caring leads to a further step—sharing. It's a powerful prayer and action combination.

Jesus also taught that *fruitful action leads to answered prayer.* "I

chose you and appointed you," He said, "to go and bear fruit—
fruit that will last. *Then* the Father will give you whatever you
ask in my name" (emphasis added). It's as if Jesus is saying, "The
Father is on the lookout for believers who are committed to a life
of service and obedience, and finding them He is quick to answer
their prayers." I am reminded of the words of the Old Testament
prophet who said, "The eyes of the LORD range throughout the
earth to strengthen those whose hearts are fully committed to him"
(2 Chronicles 16:9). Worldly minded pray-ers tend to look for bail-
outs. Kingdom-minded believers tend to look for ministry opportunities. God looks for and particularly blesses the fruitfulness of
kingdom-minded believers.

Asking and acting belong together. An old Latin adage, *ora et
labora,* reinforces this idea. Translated, it means "pray and work!"
The praying that precedes action must not be underemphasized.
The action that needs to follow up on prayer cannot be overempha-
sized. When we ask we move the hands of God. When we act we
become the hands of God.

Has it ever occurred to you that prayer can be dangerous? C.
Samuel Storms thinks it is. He warns, "One of the most dangerous
things about prayer is the tendency for it to become an excuse for
doing nothing."[3] Be careful when you pray, careful that your prayers
do not become an excuse for doing nothing. Instead, when you pray
be ready to report for duty!

Something to **Think** About

- Why might prayer without action be defective? Why is action
  without prayer deficient?

• Can you think of a time when your intercessory prayers led you to action? How about a time when your prayers should have led to action but didn't. What have you learned through these experiences?

• Is it okay to intercede when we know there will be no opportunity to act as, for example, in a crisis situation in a foreign country?

• How could Jesus possibly promise that the Father would give fruit-bearing Christians whatever they asked for in His name (John 15:16)? Isn't that a stretch?

Something to **Pray** About

• *Praise* God for His ability to factor our prayers into His way of ruling the world.
• *Thank* God that intercessory prayer prepares us for, leads us to, and sustains us in action.
• If you have only prayed when you could have followed through with some action, *repent* of that and seek God's forgiving grace.
• *Ask* the Holy Spirit to keep you alert to the action opportunities that come out of your prayers.
• *Commit* yourself to move the hands of God through prayer and to be the hands of God through action.

Something to **Act** On

As you intercede tell the Lord that you are willing to act if He will guide and enable you. Then watch for an opportunity and grasp it.

CHAPTER 25

The Healing Power of Prayer

"Go back and report to John what you have seen and heard: The blind receive sight, the lame walk, those who have leprosy are cured, the deaf hear, the dead are raised, and the good news is preached to the poor."
—Luke 7:22

Is anyone among you in trouble? Let them pray. Is anyone happy? Let them sing songs of praise. Is anyone among you sick? Let them call the elders of the church to pray over them and anoint them with oil in the name of the Lord. And the prayer offered in faith will make them well; the Lord will raise them up. If they have sinned, they will be forgiven. Therefore confess your sins to each other and pray for each other so that you may be healed. The prayer of a righteous person is powerful and effective. —James 5:13–16, TNIV

F ew things concern people more than their health. Our lives today are loaded with information about health foods, health fitness, health care, health insurance, and all sorts of health issues. Health is big in the church too. Health-related prayer requests dominate our church prayer times and prayer chains. Our concern about health is not all bad. Health matters to God too. It's just that His idea of health is much grander and more glorious than ours. He wants us to be healthy: mentally, emotionally, and spiritually, as well as physically. He wants us to pray, not just for physical health, but for all kinds of health.

God is a healing God. He revealed Himself to the Israelites, traveling in the wilderness, as "the LORD, who heals you" (Exodus 15:26). A little later He promised that He would keep them free from every disease (Deuteronomy 7:15). David urges us not to forget that God is a God who "heals all your diseases" (Psalm 103:3).

Jesus was the supreme healer. His life and ministry reflected the Father's heart. His healing ministry gave a clear sign of how the world should be and some day would be. Early in His ministry He responded to the question of John the Baptist's emissaries saying, "Go back and report to John what you have seen and heard: The blind receive sight, the lame walk, those who have leprosy are cured, the deaf hear, the dead are raised, and the good news is preached to the poor." Luke tells us that Jesus, anointed by God and empowered by the Holy Spirit, "went around doing good and healing all who were under the power of the devil" (Acts 10:38). Jesus was a healing Savior who cared deeply about the hurts humans suffer—hurts of the body as well as the soul.

We all need healing of one sort or another. We live in a fallen, sin-cursed world where both natural and spiritual forces operate in our sicknesses. The suffering caused by sin and by the ongoing works of the evil one touches our minds, souls, spirits, and bodies. We need to be saved from the destructive power of sin. We need to be relieved of the anxieties, fears, and scars that torment our inner worlds. We need to be delivered from the appetites and desires that drive us to compulsive, sinful behavior. We all need the healing touch of God's Holy Spirit.

God wants us to pray for healing. Prayer is a means that He uses to accomplish His will in the world today. When Jesus urged us to pray, "Give us this day our daily bread," He had in mind praying for all of our bodily needs, including health. James, the brother of Jesus, gives us a mandate for Christian healing when he says, "Is anyone among you sick? Let them call the elders of the church to pray over them and anoint them with oil in the name of the Lord." God is pleased that we want full health and that we pray for healing. It's what He wants too.

Prayers for healing make a difference. More healing takes place when we pray for healing than when we don't. It may be an inner emotional healing or a spiritual transformation. It may rally the body's natural healing powers or assist medical remedies. When the Bible says, "The prayer of a righteous person is powerful and effective," it means that God acts powerfully and effectively through the prayers of His people. We may not always get exactly what we want, but God will achieve what He wants and that is always good. God is sovereign and acts freely, yet freely binds Himself to the prayers of His people. Think of that the next time you pray healing prayers for someone.

There should be these seven steps in our approach to healing prayer. First, *praise* God as a healing God and *praise* Jesus as the supreme healer. Second, *thank* God for His past mercies and for the healing promises in His Word. Third, *confess* any known sin so that it might not hinder your healing prayers. Fourth, seek to *discern* the Spirit's direction for your healing prayers. Fifth, being sensitive to what the Spirit has revealed, *intercede* for total health—health of body, mind, and spirit. Sixth, *trust* God's gracious and wise response and be ready to receive gratefully what He chooses to give. Finally, *persist* in prayer until the answer comes or until God releases you from this prayer responsibility.

What can we expect when we pray for healing? We can be sure that God is concerned about the total health of those for whom we pray. We can expect that God will hear and act in accord with His nature and promises. We can expect that we will be healthier if we pray than if we don't pray. At the very least we can expect that the persons we pray for will experience God's wondrous love and all-sufficient grace.

Beyond these seven steps in our approach to healing prayer there remains the question: What if we pray and the person is not healed? Following are seven of the most prominent reasons why some people are not physically healed when we pray:

Lack of faith. The Bible presents faith as an important factor in healing—the faith of the person praying and the faith of the person receiving prayer. Jesus often ministered healing in response to faith (Matthew 9:29). Sometimes His work was impeded because people lacked faith (Matthew 13:58). Jesus still works in response to faith.

Unconfessed sin. Unconfessed sin can hinder healing (James 5:16). Jesus' healing often involved forgiveness of sin (Mark 2:5; John 5:14). Those who are praying for the healing of others should examine their own lives lest a cherished sin hinder their prayers. Those being prayed for should also search their hearts and lives to make sure that unconfessed sin is not a hindrance to God's working.

Lack of persistence. Some of God's healings are instantaneous; some are delayed; some are gradual (Mark 8:22–25). Persistent prayer is essential in the ministry of healing.

Faulty diagnosis. If the diagnosis is wrong, we may be looking and praying for the wrong solution. We may be looking for physical healing when the need is for inner healing. We may be looking for inner healing when the need is for deliverance from an evil spirit. It's important to pray about the real problem.

Neglect of the right means. While we are praying for supernatural intervention, God may want to impart health through diet, exercise, adequate sleep, or weight control. Physicians and medicines are also gifts from God for healing. We cannot neglect the means God has given us for health.

Not the right time. God is the master of timing. The writer of Ecclesiastes reminds us that God "has made everything beautiful in its time" (3:11). God may have good reasons to delay the healing you are praying for.

Higher purpose. From God's perspective physical health is not the highest value. He sometimes permits suffering in order to accomplish a greater glory (Romans 8:18). He may allow grief in order to refine our faith (1 Peter 1:7). He may use trials to bring us to spiritual maturity (James 1:3–4). He may also be using a sickness to graduate a person to glory. When you are praying for healing, watch for God's higher purposes.

God's answers to our healing prayers will always reflect His goodness and grace. God cares more than we can imagine. We don't have to convince Him to care. And in His caring He wants what is best for us. He stands ready to deliver us from the evil one and the afflictions that the devil may bring upon us. Though He does not always heal our physical diseases in response to prayer, He always sends sustaining grace and makes His power perfect in our weakness (2 Corinthians 12:8–9).

Something to **Think** About

- What kinds of healing have you already experienced? What kinds of healing might you still need to receive?

- What kind of "healing" do unconverted persons need? Emotionally scarred persons? Angry persons?

- What kinds of health might God be working out in a person's life when He chooses not to grant physical healing?

Something to **Pray** About

- *Praise* God as a healing God.
- *Thank* God for the many ways that He has healed you and others for whom you have prayed.
- If sin has kept God from giving you the health He wants for you, *confess* that to the Lord and seek His cleansing grace.
- *Ask* God to heal anything in you that needs healing—emotional, spiritual, or physical.
- *Intercede* for emotional, spiritual, and physical health for family, friends, and others whom God lays on your heart.

Something to **Act** On

Practice the seven approach-to-healing-prayer steps mentioned in this chapter when you pray for the health of others.

CHAPTER 26

When the God Who Answers Doesn't

Your iniquities have separated you from your God; your sins have hidden his face from you, so that he will not hear. —Isaiah 59:2

If anyone turns a deaf ear to the law, even his prayers are detestable. —Proverbs 28:9

When you ask, you do not receive, because you ask with wrong motives, that you may spend what you get on your pleasures. —James 4:3

God has opened the way for all believers to come to Him confidently in prayer. He wants us to come, even urges us to come. But there are things that can hinder God from "hearing" and answering our prayers. All of the hindrances involve some sort of sin—sin in our hearts, in our lives, in our attitudes, or in our relationships. It's important for us to understand these sin hindrances and to deal with them so that nothing will block our prayers.

The Bible names several specific sin hindrances to God hearing our prayers. The first and most obvious hindrance to intercession is *unconfessed sin*. Isaiah reproached the Jews of his day, saying, "Your iniquities have separated you from your God; your sins have hidden his face from you, so that he will not hear." David understood that, if he had cherished sin in his heart, "the Lord would not have listened" (Psalm 66:18). Unconfessed sin, whether it is past or present, can hinder the prayers of the most sincere intercessor. When unconfessed sin impedes prayer, the problem is not in *what* we are asking or even *why*. The problem is in the heart of the person *who* is asking. God may be perfectly willing to give us what we ask, but our unwillingness to deal with a sin makes Him unwilling to listen. The good news, though, is that it is not *sin* that hinders our prayers, but *unconfessed sin*. Sincere confession will always remove the hindrance and restore a pure heart and prayers' true power.

Second, intercession may be hindered by *wrong motives*. James speaks clearly about the problem of wrong motives. He says, "When you ask, you do not receive, because you ask with wrong motives, that you may spend what you get on your pleasures." God doesn't mind our asking for good things for ourselves or for others, even good things that can give us joy or pleasure. He does want to meet our needs and give us joy. The issue in this case is not what we ask, but *why* we ask. If we are asking in an attempt to satisfy some sinful desire, that's a wrong motive. Such prayers simply ask God to serve us for the sake of our gratification. If, on the other hand, we are asking so that we and those we pray for can love and serve God better, that is a right motive. It puts our requests in line with God's will. God is not in the business of answering selfishly motivated prayers, but He loves to answer rightly motivated prayers. You can check your motives in prayer by asking yourself, "Why am I asking this?" and then give yourself an honest answer.

Third, our intercessory prayers can be hindered by *indifference to human need*. In His Word, God says, "If a man shuts his ears to the cry of the poor, he too will cry out and not be answered" (Proverbs 21:13). God links His willingness to hear our prayers to our willingness to hear the cries of the poor. If we are praying for God to meet the needs of the poor but are unwilling to step up to meet those needs, when and where this is possible, we should not expect God to answer. James asks us to imagine a person who, in the face of poverty, says to the needy person, "'Go, I wish you well; keep warm and well fed,' but does nothing about his physical need" (James 2:16). Such a person, says James, has no faith. Faith must be matched by actions. Prayers must also be matched with actions. God expects intercessors to be thoughtfully and lovingly involved in the lives of those with needs. If our ears are open to the cries of the poor, the cries that come from "the least, the last, and the lost," then God's ears will be open to our prayers.

Fourth, being *inconsiderate or disrespectful* in family relationships can also hinder our intercessory prayers. Peter speaks plainly to husbands when he says, "Husbands, in the same way be considerate as you live with your wives, and treat them with respect . . . so that nothing will hinder your prayers" (1 Peter 3:7). The phrase "in the same way" links these words also to wives and their relationship to their husbands. I would add that the same principle applies to parent-child relationships. If children disobey their parents or if parents embitter their children (Colossians 3:20–21), this will also hinder prayer. How we treat family members will determine how God treats our prayers. The word that Peter uses for "hinder" was originally used to describe a road that was impassable because it was broken up and barricaded so that an invading army could not pass. That's what happens to our pathway to the throne when we respond insensitively and unlovingly to those close to us. The sins that hinder family relationships also hinder our relationship with our heavenly Father.

Fifth, our prayers for others can be hampered by *lack of faith*. When the disciples were unable to free a boy from demonic seizures, they asked Jesus why they couldn't drive out the demon. In response Jesus took them to task and said, "Because you have so little faith"

(Matthew 17:20). In Mark's version of this story Jesus noted that it was also lack of prayer (Mark 9:29). In other words Jesus was saying that their efforts failed because they did not pray in faith. The Bible says simply, "Without faith it is impossible to please God" (Hebrews 11:6). Without faith it is also impossible to intercede powerfully and effectively. Prayer is not just throwing wishes toward heaven with the hope that something will happen. It is trusting that God will act in accord with His nature and His promises. Don't expect God to do anything if you pray without faith.

Finally, our intercessory prayers can be hindered by *disobedience.* Solomon, in the book of Proverbs, attributes unanswered prayer to disobedience. He says, "If anyone turns a deaf ear to the law, even his prayers are detestable." Turning a deaf ear to the law is disobedience. It's saying to God, "I'm not going to listen to you!" And God's response is, "Then I won't listen to you." On the other hand, obedience leads to answered prayer. The apostle John says, "If our hearts do not condemn us, we have confidence before God and receive from him anything we ask, because we obey his commands and do what pleases him" (1 John 3:21–22).

Developing an effective intercessory prayer life depends on having an intimate and unencumbered relationship with God. God's Word promises that "the eyes of the Lord are on the righteous and his ears are attentive to their prayer," but it warns in the same verse that "the face of the Lord is against those who do evil" (1 Peter 3:12). If you don't seem to be getting answers to your intercessory prayers, you need to look first into your own heart. Ask God to search you and to expose any sin that may be hindering your prayers. Wait silently on Him. Confess anything that He shows you. Then intercede with power and with freedom, knowing that the eyes of the Lord are on you and His ears are attentive to your prayers.

Something to **Think** About

- All of the hindrances listed above involve some sort of sin. What is there about sin that causes God to turn a deaf ear?

- Think about *why* you are praying certain things for others. Is your motive God-glorifying? What will God gain if He answers your prayer?

- What kinds of wrong behaviors by husbands, wives, parents, or children will hinder the prayers of family members? Be as specific as possible.

- What is the difference between prayers that throw wishes toward heaven and prayers of faith?

Something to **Pray** About

- *Praise* God for His right ways of responding to our prayers, even if that means He doesn't respond until we deal with sin.
- *Thank* God for revealing the hindrances to prayer so clearly in the Bible.
- *Ask* God to reveal any hindrances to prayer that may exist in your life.
- *Confess* any prayer hindrances that the Spirit reveals to you and seek God's forgiveness.
- *Commit* yourself to regularly check for and deal with sins that may hinder your prayers.

Something to **Act** On

Check the motives behind your intercessory prayers for the next couple weeks by regularly asking yourself, "How will God be glorified if He grants this request?"

CHAPTER 27

When Life Conspires Against Prayer

Then he returned to his disciples and found them sleeping. "Could you men not keep watch with me for one hour?" he asked Peter. "Watch and pray so that you will not fall into temptation. The Spirit is willing, but the body is weak." —Matthew 26:40–41

I can do everything through him who gives me strength.

—Philippians 4:13

It has been said, "The worst enemy of the best is something that is good." Prayer is one of those "best" things. There are a host of good things that conspire against prayer. Never in the history of the world has the devil had more tools in his kitbag to hinder prayer than today. In this chapter we'll look at a few of those "worst enemies," and some simple ways to deal them.

Busyness. When I invite people at a prayer seminar to name things that hinder their prayer lives, busyness is almost always the first one named. Think of the various forms of media that provide distraction: radio, television, Internet, land lines or cell phones, newspapers, magazines, advertising mail. Then there are the options that easy transportation provides: run to the bank or the store; run the kids to piano lessons, soccer practice, or a friend's house; run out for fast food; take in a ballgame, a concert, a movie. None of these are wrong in themselves. Many of them are potentially good. However, as our lives get filled with these good things, prayer easily gets crowded out.

What to do? Deliberately carve out time for prayer as a first priority, knowing how really important it is. Don Postema, author of *Space for God*, found that scheduling time for prayer by writing "Meet God" into his daily calendar, reminded him not only of the time but of the value of that time. Prayer is not just a time to quickly cast some wishes heavenward. It is a time to meet with God—relaxed, enjoyable, loving fellowship with God. Once you have set aside that time and written it into your calendar, eliminate anything in your busy schedule that is less important than meeting God.

Carnal confidence. You have probably heard the saying, "Pray as if everything depends on God; work as if everything depends on you." If we did that we would bring a well-balanced combination of prayer and work to any project or challenge. But when our modern I-can-do-it confidence kicks into gear, we tend to settle for about 90 percent human effort and 10 percent prayer. Human effort leads the way. Prayer is added as an afterthought.

What to do? First of all, remember and believe what Jesus said in John 15:5: "Apart from me you can do nothing." Then ask yourself what an all-competent, all-knowing, all-wise God could do in the project or the challenging situation you are facing. Once you have answered that question, bring God in by means of prayer. Balance your work with prayer and your prayer with work. You may discover with Paul that you "can do everything through him who gives [you] strength" (Philippians 4:13). Don't let carnal confidence keep you from bathing all your work in prayer.

Love of ease. Persevering prayer is hard work. Paul commended Epaphras as one who was "always wrestling in prayer" for the Colossians. Moses also understood wrestling prayer—wrestling as he did with God to spare the rebellious Israelites in the desert of Sinai. Wrestling isn't easy. It involves strenuous hand-to-hand effort to bring an opponent to the ground. Most Christians find wrestling in prayer too difficult. We tend to prefer the more effortless and comfortable forms of service. Jesus chided the three disciples who twice fell asleep when they should have been supporting Him as He wrestled through a painful night in Gethsemane. Jesus' words to the disciples challenge all whose love of ease causes failure in prayer. "Watch and pray," He said, "so that you will not fall into temptation. The spirit is willing, but the body is weak" (Matthew 26:40–41). God Himself, through His Spirit, can help us overcome our love of ease and the weakness of the flesh.

Worldly values. We pray for what we value. Epaphras wrestled hard in prayer for the Colossians that they might "stand firm in all the will of God, mature and fully assured" (4:12). That's what he wanted for his friends in Christ more than anything else. How much do you want those kinds of things for the believers you pray for? If we want spiritual riches more than anything else for our friends and loved ones, then we will be motivated to pray fervently for those kinds of things. If, however, what we value most for them are things like worldly success, wealth, prosperity, pleasurable experiences, and creature comforts, then we are not likely to pray like Epaphras did.

What's the corrective? If we value for others the best that God has for them—things like grace, faith, hope, love, wisdom, spiritual maturity, and the fruit of the Spirit (Galatians 5:22–23), then we will labor in prayer for the spiritual well-being of those we pray for just like Epaphras did. Our prayers will be an overflow of our inward desires.

False prayer. False prayer can hinder true prayer. Many prayers today are simply rote recitations that come from empty hearts. They are pious sounding words without passion and with little thought of God. They may sound like prayer. The person uttering them may feel like he or she has prayed, but they are no more prayers than the words of a parrot who has learned to say, "Praise the Lord!" They are like the vain street-corner prayers of the Pharisees condemned by Jesus (Matthew 6:5). False prayers of this kind conspire against true prayer by making people think that they have prayed when they really haven't.

How can we get beyond false prayer? True prayer is a two-way conversation with a Person. It begins with a consciousness of God. If we are not conscious of that Person, we are not in a conversation and we are not praying. Being conscious of the Person to whom we are speaking when we are praying may require stopping, mediating, listening, and asking God to take the initiative and to break through to our conscious mind. It also means praying from the heart; saying what we really feel and really think, not just words that come to mind or words that someone else has provided.

It is true that life today conspires against prayer. However, the Holy Spirit, our indwelling prayer assistant, is greater than the conspiracies of life that hinder our praying. He is able to help us pray as we ought. Twice in the New Testament we are encouraged to "pray in the Spirit," by which the authors mean "pray as enabled by the Spirit." Never let life conspire to keep you from praying as you should. Instead, trust the Spirit to help you pray as God wants you to pray.

Something to **Think** About

• What are some of the differences between a merely mouthed prayer and a heartfelt-desire prayer?

- Why might writing "Meet God" in your daily calendar, in order to schedule a daily prayer time, help you become serious about using that devotional time?

- What is there about carnal confidence that tends to keep us from praying?

- What can the Holy Spirit do to help you overcome each one of the hindrances mentioned above? Be specific.

Something to **Pray** About

- *Praise* the Holy Spirit for His thorough understanding of prayer and His ability to help us pray as we ought.
- Think of some heroes of prayer whose prayer lives are recorded in scripture, and *give thanks* for the testimony of their lives.
- If you have succumbed to one or more of the prayer hindrances mentioned above, *confess* that failure and receive God's pardon.
- *Ask* for the Holy Spirit's help to avoid the prayer traps and pitfalls of our world.
- Discern, with the Spirit's help, the best time and place for private prayer and make a definite *commitment* to that time.

Something to **Act** On

Schedule a specific daily prayer time by writing "Meet God" in your daily calendar. Think about the One whom you are meeting at that time and the enjoyment you will have in meeting Him. Remember that He will enjoy meeting you too.

CHAPTER 28

Mistakes Intercessors Make

"And when you pray, do not be like the hypocrites, for they love to pray standing in the synagogues and on the street corners to be seen by men. I tell you the truth, they have received their reward in full. . . . And when you pray, do not keep on babbling like pagans, for they think they will be heard because of their many words. Do not be like them."

—Matthew 6:5, 7–8

The mother of Zebedee's sons came to Jesus with her sons and, kneeling down, asked a favor of him.

"What is it you want?" he asked.

She said, "Grant that one of these two sons of mine may sit at your right and the other at your left in your kingdom."

"You don't know what you are asking," Jesus said to them.

—Matthew 20:20–22

Mistakes can easily lead to confusion and frustration. When I try to use the fifty buttons on the remote that controls our home entertainment system, I often get it wrong. The problem is that I simply don't know how they all work. My mistakes lead to frustration. Intercessory prayer can be like that too. Mistaken notions about how intercession works can easily lead to frustration with prayer and disappointment with God.

Following are seven mistakes intercessors make and some ways to avoid them.

Mistake 1: Praying to impress others. Jesus censored the spiritual hypocrites of His day for praying on street corners "to be seen by men." Praying on street corners is not a problem in Western cultures today. However, praying showy prayers in small groups or prayer meetings in order to impress others just might amount to the same thing. I find that it is all too easy, when praying in a group, to be so conscious of what others think of my prayers that I am barely conscious of God. That's a mistake. "Don't pray showy prayers to impress others," Jesus is saying. "You might impress some people that way and get their approval, but you won't impress God."

Mistake 2: Trying to twist God's arm. It is not uncommon for us to try and turn intercession into a way to get special favors from God. And when God seems reluctant to cooperate, we put the pressure on. We'd like Him to serve us, to fit into our plans. The mother of the sons of Zebedee tried that. She had a plan for her sons and so she said to Jesus, "Grant that one of these two sons of mine [James and John] may sit at your right and the other at your left in your kingdom." She thought she could get her plan to work by twisting Jesus' arm. But it didn't work. Jesus turned her down. He had another plan to think about—the Father's kingdom plan. Intercession is not about getting God to do what we want. It is about God getting us involved in His kingdom plans by means of our prayers.

Mistake 3: Words without thought. Saying prayers is not necessarily praying. There are lots of intercessory pleas uttered that are not really prayers at all. They are non-prayers, not because the words are not right, but because the words are without heart. They are words spoken without a thought of God. E. M. Bounds calls them "prayerless prayers." The babbling prayers of the pagans who thought to impress God with "their many words" (Matthew 6:7–8) were prayerless prayers. "Do not be like them," Jesus said. Christians sometimes offer prayerless prayers too—mindless prayers, rote phrases uttered without thought of God. Even a quick rattling off of the Lord's Prayer can be a prayerless prayer. "Don't pray like that," Jesus would say. Pray with an awareness of God. Have a conversation with Him that is heart to heart.

Mistake 4: Habits without heart. In the Western world prayer often comes with certain prayer habits like folding our hands, closing our eyes, bowing our heads, saying "thee" and "thou," and ending with "for Jesus' sake, amen." Prayer habits certainly have their value. They may in fact help us pray. But they are not the essence of prayer. We may use all of these habits, and utter beautiful words that sound like prayers, and still not be praying. Prayer habits may, in fact, lead us to believe that we have done it right, and that God must surely be pleased, when the opposite is true. We may simply be going through motions. Prayer doesn't work because we do it correctly. Prayer works when we have a heart-to-heart connection with God. The issue is not getting prayer right; it is getting to the right Person.

Mistake 5: Foxhole praying. In war years military people talked about foxhole praying. They meant that when a soldier is dug into a foxhole and bullets are flying all around, the natural inclination is to pray. It's natural to turn to God in an emergency. And that is the way it should be. God wants us to come to Him with our troubles. James said, "Is any one of you in trouble? He should pray" (James 5:13). But the value of prayer goes far beyond "foxholes." We make a mistake when we fail to go on interceding when times smooth out and there is no emergency. Scripture urges us to pray "on all occasions with all kinds of prayers and requests" and to "always keep on praying for all the saints" (Ephesians 6:18). Jesus prayed for nonemergency things like faith, unity, and spiritual protection. He taught us to pray proactively for the Father's glory, kingdom, and purposes on earth. Almost all of Paul's intercessory prayers were forward-looking, life-transforming prayers for things like fruitfulness, spiritual growth, wisdom, empowerment, and sanctification. God has given us intercession, not just for emergencies, but so that we can pray down His blessings on our family members, friends, fellow believers, neighbors, and our world.

Mistake 6: Talking but not listening. Intercession is not just one-way asking; it's a two-way conversation with God. It's dialogue, not monologue. It involves listening to God as well as talking to God. To intercede correctly we have to be conscious of the Person we are talking to and aware of His plan and His purposes. All true prayer, including intercession, starts with God. If that is the case, then intercession must start with seeking to know how God wants us to pray, and then lead to prayer in line with His will. God is ready and willing to facilitate our intercession by making His will known to us. He has given us His Word and His Spirit to help us know His will.

Mistake 7: Mistaking God's promises. When lifted out of context, some of the prayer promises in scripture seem unlimited. Take, for example, Jesus' promise to pray-ers in the Sermon on the Mount: "Ask and it will be given to you; seek and you will find; knock and the door will opened to you. For everyone who asks receives; he who seeks finds; and to him who knocks, the door will be opened" (Matthew 7:7–8). That's an incredible promise, and one that we should be claiming regularly, but it is not as unlimited as it may seem. It is not an open-ended, blank-check promise. The words and the context clearly set limits to Jesus' promise. First, it's limited to believers. Jesus was teaching disciples. Second, it's limited to asking for ourselves: "It will be given to *you* . . . *you* will find . . . the door will be opened to *you*" (emphasis added). And third, its focus is on the spiritual help believers need to live by the standards in the Sermon on the Mount. Persons who attempt to claim this promise, or other seemingly unlimited promises, without recognizing the limits will be disappointed and may even begin to doubt the veracity of God's Word.

Be careful not to let mistaken notions sidetrack your intercessory prayer life. Let scripture guide you in knowing and practicing true and valid biblical principles of intercessory prayer. Here are the positive alternatives to the mistaken notions above.

Intercessors pray to an audience of One, not for the ears people who may hear them.

Intercessors take hold of God's willingness; they don't twist His arm.

True prayer is a heart-to-heart talk with God, not mouthing pious sounding phrases.

True prayer is not getting it right; it is getting to the right Person.

Intercession is for all times, not just tough times.

Intercession requires listening to God, not just asking.

God's prayer promises are beyond measure, but they are not unlimited.

Something to **Think** About

- Which, if any, of the mistaken notions mentioned in this chapter affect your prayer life? Which ones have you noticed in others?

- What healthy prayer practices could help believers avoid mistakes in intercession?

- How can believers get beyond the emergency mode of intercession?

- Why is listening to God so basic to effective intercession?

Something to **Pray** About

- *Praise* God for the hearing ear that He has tuned to our prayers.
- *Thank* God for giving us clear and positive guidelines for intercessory prayer.
- *Confess* any failure that you have become aware of in your intercessory prayer life.
- *Ask* God to help you be an effective intercessor.
- *Commit* yourself to becoming a faithful, powerful intercessor.

Something to **Act** On

Pick one area of your intercessory prayer life that you know needs improvement and work on that. Share with someone else what problem you are working on and what you are doing about it.

CHAPTER 29

Practical Steps for Effective Intercession

*"Be still, and know that I am God; I will be exalted among the nations, I will be exalted in the earth." —*Psalm 46:10

*Search me, O God, and know my heart; test me and know my anxious thoughts. See if there is any offensive ways in me, and lead me in the way everlasting. —*Psalm 139:23–24

*"If you . . . know how to give good gifts to your children, how much more will the Father in heaven give the Holy Spirit to those who ask him!" —*Luke 11:13

Andrew Murray writes: "Every art unfolds its secrets and its beauty only to the man who practices it. To the humble soul who prays in the obedience of faith, who practices prayer and intercession diligently because God asks it, the secret of the Lord will be revealed."[1] I hope and pray that by now you have gained many helpful insights into intercession. Though you have probably practiced a number of intercessory prayer activities along the way, I think it will still be useful to end with a final chapter focusing specifically on practical steps for intercession.

Here are ten practical steps for effective intercession.

First, *make time for intercessory prayer.* If prayer is to be a priority, then we must make time for it. Those who try haphazardly to find some time each day for prayer will time and again be frustrated. Effective intercession begins with good planning. Plan for a daily time, a quiet place, and a purposeful way to use that time. Be willing to give up other priorities in order to preserve that time. E. M. Bounds was probably right when he said: "God does not bestow his gifts on the casual or hasty comers and goers. Much time with God alone is the secret of knowing him and of influence with him."[2] Plan well and make meeting God the highlight of your day. Of course, since God is with you in all of life, you can pray anytime and anywhere.

Second, *seek God's face before you seek His hand*. Start your prayer time being quiet before God. Invite Him to reveal Himself to you. Begin to listen for His voice. Discover His heart. Feel His presence. Let him express His love for you, and express your love for Him. Ask Him to help you see things from His point of view. Faith grows strong when you focus on God. Draw near to God and He will draw near to you. "Be still," He said, "and know that I am God" (Psalm 46:10). Inner stillness, together with freedom from external distractions, paves the way to experiencing God.

Third, *make sure your heart is clean*. Unconfessed sin will block prayer (Psalm 66:18). Invite God to search you as David did when he said, "Search me, O God, and know my heart; test me and know my anxious thoughts. See if there is any offensive way in me" (Psalm 139:23–24). That's a prayer that God is ready to answer. He is eager to help us identify and confess sin so that He can cleanse us and free us from its burden and its guilt. Clearing the air with God, by means of confession, allows us to go forward in prayer without hindrance.

Fourth, *ask for the Spirit's help*. Without the Spirit's help we cannot pray as we ought to (Romans 8:26). With His help we can be the effective intercessors God intends us to be. Jesus said, "How much more [than earthly parents] will your Father in heaven give the Holy Spirit to those who ask him!" (Luke 11:13). The Father is eager to give the Spirit because He knows how much we need the Spirit's help, and He wants us to be effective intercessors. God's part is to offer and to give the Spirit. Our part is to claim the gift.

Fifth, *stop and listen to God.* True prayer is dialog not monologue, so in prayer we have to listen as well as talk. That's true even in intercession. By listening to God speak through His Word and by His Spirit, we receive direction in what and how to pray for others. Listening might mean using the great prayers of the Bible and inserting the names of people we know into them. Listening might mean that the Holy Spirit will call to mind a promise, a warning, a command, or an example that gives direction to our prayers. It might mean that the Spirit will burden you to pray a specific prayer, for a specific person, at a specific time. When we stop and listen we are inviting God to direct our thoughts and our prayers. With His direction we can't go wrong. He is an expert at prayer.

Sixth, *pray with expectant faith.* The faith we bring to intercession is not confidence in prayer, it is confidence in God. It is being absolutely sure "that he exists, and that he rewards those who earnestly seek him" (Hebrews 11:6). That God "rewards" means that He hears our prayers, takes them seriously, and answers on the basis of His wisdom and His will. He does not promise to do everything we ask. He will always answer in a way that brings Him glory, advances His kingdom, and works for our good. The faith we need to be effective intercessors comes as a gift from God, so it too is something we must ask for.

Seventh, *pray for increased love.* Love is the motivating force in all true intercessory prayer. We intercede because we love. Love always wants to give, to help, and to bless. It is even willing to sacrifice self in order to see another person receive the riches of Christ. When we pray we step with God into His loving concern for those we pray for. Ask God to grow your capacity to love as you intercede for your family, your friends, and your world.

Eighth, *persist in prayer.* As you persist in prayer one of three things may happen. First, the answer may come. That's, of course, your signal to stop praying. In Jesus' story of the friend at midnight who knocks persistently on his neighbor's door, the neighbor eventually comes to the door and gives him bread. He has his answer and he stops knocking (Luke11:5–8). Second, God may say "no." If He says "no," it's time to stop asking. Paul prayed for the removal of his thorn in the flesh. When God denied his request and promised His all-sufficient grace instead, Paul's stopped asking (2 Corinthians 12:1–10). Third, God may lift the prayer burden. When God, who *gives* prayer burdens, *lifts* the burden, it is time to stop praying. It means that God has heard enough and He is redirecting your prayer energies. If God, however, doesn't give you reason to stop, it probably means He wants you to persist in asking. Whatever you do, be sensitive to God's working and timing as you persist in prayer.

Ninth, *be ready to take action.* God wants more from us than just asking. When we intercede, we will often find ourselves identifying with those for whom we are praying and becoming eager to help them. That may be a call to action. If you feel such a call, ask God what He wants you to do for that person or in that situation, and offer yourself as a channel through whom He can work.

Tenth, *find one or more prayer partners.* There is a time and place to pray alone. There is also great benefit in praying with others. Prayer partners can give us support and encouragement in intercessory prayer. Your partner may be your spouse, another family member, a fellow church member, or a neighbor. You can keep in touch by e-mail, pray together by phone, or find a convenient time and place to meet. Learn to listen when your prayer partners pray and pray with them. Find a pattern of praying together that is comfortable for everyone involved.

Intercession is important work. God intends *our* work of intercession to facilitate *His* work of building the kingdom. Intercession works when we are willing to work at it. Ole Hallesby reminds us: "It is our Lord's will that we who have received access to these powers through prayer, should go through this world transmitting heavenly power to every corner of the world which needs it sorely. Our lives should be, according to our Lord's plans, quiet but steadily flowing streams of blessing, which through our prayers and intercessions should reach our whole environment."[3] I pray that God may use you and those with whom you pray in that way.

Something to **Think** About

- What tends to happen when a person's prayer time starts by seeking God's face before seeking His hand? What if we just start by seeking God's hand?

- Which of the above practical steps are you already doing? Which of the steps would you like to develop?

- What would you like to do with the prayer power God has given you? Do you have a sense that your intercessory prayers are transmitting heavenly power to places in the world where that power is sorely needed?

Something to **Pray** About

- *Praise* God for working so faithfully and powerfully in response to your prayers.
- *Thank* God for the gift of intercession and for all the prayer help He gives you.
- *Confess* your failings in intercession and claim the grace of God's forgiveness for these failings.
- *Ask* God for all you need to be the intercessor He wants you to be: a clean heart, the Spirit's help, a listening ear, an expectant faith, a heart of love, the strength to persist, the willingness to act, and prayer partners.
- *Commit* yourself to the labor of intercession.

Something to **Act** On

Work thoughtfully through the ten practical steps for effective intercession, and add to your intercessory prayer life any element from the list that may help you be more effective.

CHAPTER 30

What God Promises to Intercessors

*Let us then approach the throne of grace with confidence, so that
we may receive mercy and find grace to help us in our time of need.*
—Hebrews 4:16

*Since we have a great priest over the house of God, let us draw near to
God with a sincere heart in full assurance of faith, having our hearts
sprinkled to cleanse us from a guilty conscience.* —Hebrews 10-21–22

*For the eyes of the Lord are on the righteous and his ears are attentive to
their prayer.* —1 Peter 3:12

When we think of intercession it is natural to think of ourselves. After all we are the ones doing the intercession. We
are the ones who want things from God. It is critically important,
however, for us to think of intercession from God's perspective. Intercession is all about God. He conceived of intercession in the first
place. He asks us to pray. He makes it possible for us to pray through
the work of His Son and His Spirit. And He is committed to carry
on His work on earth in response to the prayers of His people.

God has made some incredible promises that are meant to encourage us in prayer. First, God promises to receive us as *a Father
receives a beloved child.* Jesus taught us to address God as "Our Father."
A loving Father-child relationship stands at the very center of prayer.

Awareness of the Father's love is the first and most important lesson for all pray-ers. In prayer we come to a Father who loves us and cares for us, who is interested in us and is committed to providing for us and protecting us. We come knowing that we are His children and He is our "Abba." We know it because we have "received the Spirit of sonship. And by him we cry, 'Abba, Father'" (Romans 8:15). We go to God in prayer, not first of all to get something, but to enjoy our love relationship with the Father.

And we go to Him knowing that He is no ordinary Father. He is our Father *in heaven*. He is the almighty, all-wise, sovereign God of the universe. Nothing is hidden from Him; nothing is too difficult for him. He is fully capable of hearing and answering prayer. We go to Him with childlike trust, assured that every request we make is heard and that His answers are always best.

Second, God promises to *cleanse us by the blood of Christ* so that we can come to Him. The Bible invites us to "draw near to God with a sincere heart in full assurance of faith, having our hearts sprinkled to cleanse us from a guilty conscience." The heart cleansing of Christ is what makes it possible for us to draw near to God. Sin by its very nature separates us from God and hinders prayer. Without heart cleansing we could never enter the throne room. The cleansing removes the barrier and admits us into the presence of God.

Third, God promises *the Holy Spirit to help us pray*. God understands how difficult prayer is for us and knows that "we do not know what we ought to pray." To help us pray He has given us the Spirit, who "helps us in our weakness" (Romans 8:26). The Spirit is our indwelling prayer assistant. He knows everything there is to know about prayer. He can give us the faith we need to pray, the compassion, the boldness, the persistence. He can help us with the content of our prayers and the words. As a member of the Trinity, He can help us pray in accord with God's will and in Jesus' name. He can help us avoid the mistakes that we are prone to make in prayer. God provides this matchless indwelling prayer assistant for us because He wants us to be effective intercessors. Effective intercessors are part of His perfect plan to release His power, build His kingdom, and accomplish His will on earth.

Fourth, God promises us *entrance to His throne room.* He invites us to "approach the throne of grace with confidence, so that we may receive mercy and find grace to help us in our time of need." Every true believer is welcome in the throne room. We can come with complete confidence. The door is always open. We don't even have to knock. He is expecting us. He is glad when we come. As I say in *Love to Pray,* "This wonderful welcome is extended to us not because we are worthy in ourselves. The truth is we deserve to be bared from God's presence because of our sins. But Christ has dealt with our sins and made us acceptable to God. We have been adopted as sons and daughters. We have a place in the royal family."[1]

Fifth, God promises *to be attentive to our prayers.* Peter, quoting David's words from Psalm 34, reminds us, "The eyes of the Lord are on the righteous and his ears are attentive to their prayer" (1 Peter 3:12). What an amazing promise. What a difference it will make in our prayer lives if we always come to the Father with complete assurance that He is attentive to our prayers. Nothing escapes His notice. He doesn't miss a word. He knows exactly what we mean even if we can't find the words to express it. He knows the persons we are praying for and the situations in their lives that we are referring too. Nothing is too complicated for Him to grasp. He is attentive because He desires to act in response to our prayers. His eyes are on us and He listens to us because of who we are. We are "the righteous" who have been made righteous in Jesus Christ.

Sixth, God promises to *carry on His work on earth in response to our prayers*. That has always been His way of working. God parted the Red Sea, provided for His people in forty years of wilderness journeys, and gave them victory over their enemies because Moses prayed (Exodus 17:8–13). God caused the walls of Jericho to fall down and the sun to stand still because Joshua prayed. God caused rain to stop falling for three-and-a-half years in Israel and then to fall again because Elijah prayed (James 5:16). God gave the New Testament church evangelistic zeal and miraculous signs and wonders because they prayed (Acts 4:23–31). God delivered Paul and gave him gracious favor because the Corinthian church prayed (2 Corinthians 1:10–11). That will always be God's way of working. That's our assurance as we go to Him in prayer. God shapes history, even the mini-histories of our lives, by our prayers.

Seventh, God promises that *as we pray, the devil's designs will be thwarted*. Prayer has always been a part of Christ's devil-destroying plan. He came "to destroy the devil's work" (1 John 3:8) and to see Satan crushed under our feet (Romans 16:20). Demons were cast out because of prayer (Mark 9:29). Peter's faith did not fail and the disciples were protected from the evil one because of prayer (Luke 22:23–24; John 17:11, 15). Saints were strengthened to stand in the face of the devil's attack because of prayer (Ephesians 6:18). The devil-destroying work of Christ is still in process, and prayer is a key part of it. God is delighted when, in our prayers, we stand with Him against the devil's schemes and the active "forces of evil in the heavenly realms" (Ephesians 6:12). In response to our prayers He pursues His plan to bring an end to evil.

Next time you pray, stop to remember these assurances of God. Remember that it is your loving and all-powerful Father that meets you in the throne room. Remember that you come cleansed by the blood of Christ and that you are able to pray by the help of the Holy Spirit. Remember that He welcomes you and is attentive to your prayers. Remember that He is 100 percent committed to achieving His purposes and destroying the devil's works in response to the prayers of believers just like you. I have found that remembering these things always strengthens my intercessory prayer life and encourages me to be faithful. I am sure that it will be the same for you. Stand on the promises of God, and be the intercessor God wants you to be.

Something to **Think** About

- Which one of the promises mentioned in this chapter means the most to you right now? Why?

- Why might awareness of the Father's love be considered the first and most important lesson for all pray-ers?

- Do you think that the Father is attentive even to our off-target prayers? Explain.

- What work is God carrying on right now on earth because you are interceding?

Something to **Pray** About

- *Praise* God as a promise-making, promise-keeping God.
- *Thank* God for each one of the promises He has made to you as an intercessor.

- *Ask* God to help you remember His incredible promises each time you pray.
- *Commit* yourself to the kind of intercession that will facilitate God's ongoing work in the lives of your family and friends, your church, and your world.

Something to **Act** On

In the coming weeks review the seven promises God makes to prayers. Ask God to install His perspective on intercessory prayer permanently in your heart and mind.

Endnotes

PREFACE

1. Watchman Nee, *Let Us Pray* (New York: Christian Fellowship Publishers, 1977), 3.
2. Ole Hallesby, *Prayer* (Minneapolis: Augsburg, 1959), 164.

CHAPTER 3

1. E. M. Bounds, *The Complete Works* (Grand Rapids, MI: Baker, 1990), 257.
2. Mother Teresa, *Seeking the Heart of God* (San Francisco: Harper, 1991), 14.

CHAPTER 4

1. Dutch Sheets, *Intercessory Prayer* (Ventura, CA: Regal, 1996), 95–96.

CHAPTER 5

1. William Barclay, *The Promise of the Spirit* (London: Epworth Press, 1960), 104.
2. Hallesby, *Prayer*, 127–128.

CHAPTER 7

1. S. D. Gordon, *Quiet Talks on Prayer* (Westwood, NJ: Revell, 1967), 11.
2. Hallesby, *Prayer*, 80, 159.

CHAPTER 8

1. Darrell W. Johnson, *Fifty-Seven Words that Change the World* (Vancouver, BC: Regent College Publishing, 2005), 20.

CHAPTER 13

1. Eugene Peterson, *Working the Angles* (Grand Rapids, MI: Eerdmans, 1987), 39.

CHAPTER 18

1. Helmut Thielecki, *Our Heavenly Father* (New York:, Harper, 1960), 109.
2. Eugene Peterson, *Where Your Treasure Is* (Grand Rapids, MI: Eerdmans, 1985), 6.

CHAPTER 19

1. Andrew Murray, *With Christ in the School of Prayer* (Grand Rapids, MI: Zondervan, 1983), 75.

CHAPTER 20

1. *The Kneeling Christian* (Grand Rapids, MI: Zondervan, 1986), 17.
2. Wesley Duewel, *Touch the World Through Prayer* (Grand Rapids, MI: Francis Asbury Press, 1986), 208.

CHAPTER 22

1. Richard C. Trench, quoted in *The Encyclopedia of Religious Quotations*, ed. and comp. Frank S. Mead (Westwood, NJ: Revell, 1965), 348.
2. Andrew Murray, *Ministry of Intercession* (Minneapolis: Bethany House, 1981), 38.
3. Wesley Duewel, *Mighty Prevailing Prayer* (Grand Rapids, MI: Francis Asbury Press, 1990), 210.

CHAPTER 24

1. Jim Wallis, "The Work of Prayer," *Sojourners Magazine*, March 1979, 3.
2. C. Samuel Storms, *Reaching God's Ear* (Wheaton, IL: Tyndale House, 1988), 101.
3. Storms, *Reaching God's Ear,* 99.

CHAPTER 29

1. Murray, *Ministry of Intercession*, 92.
2. E. M. Bounds, *Complete Works,* 460.
3. Hallesby, *Prayer,* 64.

CHAPTER 30

1. Alvin VanderGriend, *Love to Pray* (Terre Haute, IN: PrayerShop Publishing, 2003), 16.

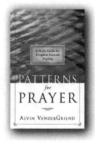